TREASURES

in the

DARKNESS

L. LAWRENCE BRANDON

LETTING GO *of* PAIN
HOLDING ON *to* FAITH

TREASURES

in the

DARKNESS

Abingdon Press
NASHVILLE

To my mother, Helen B. Lyons. Legally, the world says you are my great aunt. Heaven and I would say you are my momma. You raised me from infancy to manhood, and I'll forever be grateful to the Lord for you. You took me to church, you led me to Jesus Christ, and you taught me that earth has no sorrow heaven cannot heal—and for that, I thank you. I dedicate this book to you.

To my son, Larry Lawrence Brandon, III. I also dedicate this work to you because you will forever be in my memory. Not a day goes by that I don't think about you. Good night, Larry. Rest well. I'll see you in the morning.

CONTENTS

INTRODUCTION

I want to invite you on a journey of faith, one that reveals the love of God and how He can help you overcome private pain. What is private pain? It is severe emotional and mental distress that, for one reason or another, you keep to yourself. Many things in life can cause private pain. We all experience it at one time or another, especially when we lose someone or something that's very important to us.

Of course, losses happen for a variety of reasons. It could be that someone close to you has passed away. Maybe you've gone through a painful divorce and have been separated from your children. Perhaps you've lost your job or business. The list goes on and on.

Private pain from suffering a loss leads to experiencing

grief, which often results in going through a common psychological process called the grief cycle. During this process, you go through different stages of mourning until you come through on the other side. It's important for you to understand how this process works, so you can fully release your pain and keep moving forward with your life.

It's also essential for you to understand how, especially when you're hurting, you can still trust God and have hope for the future. Something happens to us psychologically when we love God, yet we are hit with hardships and trials we can't make sense of or have long-term needs that go unfulfilled. We ask ourselves why we have to go through these things at all. Why does God allow them?

I encourage you: No matter what it takes, hold on to your faith in God. Moving out of faith can be a subtle process. Staying in faith is a vital part of releasing your pain, coming all the way through the grief process, and fulfilling your God-given destiny. Now, if by chance you're not certain you've received Jesus Christ as your personal Savior, then it's vital for you to receive Him so you can be fully restored. Jesus cares for you more than you know.

We all have issues. We have all been challenged, yet we're all different. Everyone has his or her own fingerprints, even identical twins. But private pain is like a bullet. It has no gender, ethnic group, or race. Pain doesn't discriminate. It doesn't matter if you're wealthy or poor, young or old, male or female. Pain is pain. So we must remember: though each of us experiences and handles private pain in different ways, we must all come through the grief process.

If you feel trapped and isolated in your pain, then let me encourage you. You're not alone. There is hope and help for you.

In this book, we will look honestly at our own hearts and closely at the Bible to see how everyday people handled private pain and grief. Sometimes they did well. Other times, they fell into presumption when their faith was put to the test and they tried to move ahead without asking for God's guidance. I trust you'll see yourself many times as we move through the chapters. So relax and allow yourself room to learn from their experiences. We will also examine many practical ways you can work through your pain. You'll find a Faith Check section at the end of every chapter so you can monitor your progress.

As we move forward, I encourage you to stretch, to open your heart and mind, and to be willing to see things differently, especially if you've been actively involved in church life. Sometimes we grow up with preconceived notions, and this is especially true in the church. We often tend to adapt to our culture, and the church is a subculture that has its own church lingo.

From a pastoral perspective, I'd also like to help churches create an environment of trust, where people can admit they're suffering from some type of pain that may be private to them, without being judged. Too often, we put on "public masks" and pretend that everything is fine because we feel it's culturally acceptable. It's time for the masks to come off. We all have spots and blemishes; we all deal with private pain.

Sadly, there are some churches where the leader has issues, but masks it, fearing he or she will be rejected and ousted. If this is you, then I encourage you to keep reading. God wants you to stay in faith so you can let go of private pain and be restored. As God's people, we need to hold on to faith and release our pain so we can begin to stand as the church visible that God has called us to be.

As we prepare to start our journey, I want you to understand: though you may never get over your loss, you can overcome it. Grief is a normal part of life. However, we can have victory over our pain through faith in Jesus Christ. So hold on to your faith! You can overcome those depressing feelings that are trying to overwhelm you. You can take the Band-Aids off your wounds and let the healing process begin.

Now let's move forward.

CHAPTER 1

THE TREASURE WITHIN YOU

You Have the Light of Life

In Him was life, and the life was the light of men.

JOHN 1:4

Before we get into exposing private pain and coming all the way through the grief process, I want to look at the promise. Because when you're in pain—emotionally, physically, or otherwise—it's important not to lose sight of hope. No matter what you may be facing there is a light inside of you: a treasure that can never be taken away.

What is this treasure within you? John 1:1-4 says:

In the beginning was the Word, and the Word was with

God, and the Word was God. He was in the beginning with God. All things were made through Him, and without Him nothing was made that was made. In Him was life, and the life was the *light of men* [emphasis mine].

Second Corinthians 4:6-7 adds:

For it is the God who commanded light to shine out of darkness, who has shone in our hearts to give the light of the knowledge of the glory of God in the face of Jesus Christ. *But we have this treasure in earthen vessels*, that the excellence of the power may be of God and not of us [emphasis mine].

As we begin this journey, letting go of pain and holding on to faith, I encourage you to remember that God is going to see you all the way through to healing and victory. There is a light, a treasure, within you through your relationship with Jesus Christ that empowers you to stand, endure, and overcome for the glory of God.

Remembering this is vitally important, because when you experience loss it can be easy to focus on your pain and take your eyes off of God and His promises. And that's exactly what the enemy wants you to do. But God! He has already made a way for you to let go of your pain, hold on to your faith, and shine brightly in the darkness.

An ancient poet wrote: *Finis origine pendet*, "The end depends upon the beginning."[1] Since that time, people from almost every walk of life have repeated this phrase because it's absolutely true. Why? God established the principle. He set everything in place for light to overcome darkness. Genesis 1:1-4 says:

> In the beginning God created the heavens and the earth. The earth was without form, and void; and darkness was upon the face of the deep. And the Spirit of God was hovering over the face of the waters. Then God said, "Let there be light"; and there was light. And God saw the light, that it was good; and God divided the light from the darkness.

Of course, when God divided light from darkness He created day and night in the physical realm (v. 5). However, John 1:4 reminds us that God divides light from darkness within us when we belong to Him. In fact, all people—saved and unsaved—have "eternity" in our hearts; God places it inside of us (see Ecclesiastes 3:11). So, you see, there is always hope, especially when you belong to Jesus. As a child of God you can have firm hope for today and for the future because He won't leave you in the dark.

The book of Genesis also tells us that when God created man from the dust of the earth, He breathed into his nostrils the "breath of life" (2:7). It also records what happened when this first man, Adam, and his wife, Eve, fell prey to deception and ate the forbidden fruit. I'll quickly summarize. The Lord called to Adam and confronted them. Adam passed the buck to Eve, and then Eve passed blame to the serpent (3:9-13). Then Genesis 3:14-15 says:

> So the LORD God said to the serpent: "Because you have done this, you are cursed more than all cattle, and more than every beast of the field; on your belly you shall go, and you shall eat dust all the days of your life. And I will put enmity between you and the woman, and between your seed and her Seed; He shall bruise your head, and you shall bruise his heel."

After dealing with the serpent, God dealt with Eve and Adam. As a result of their sin, Eve would have pain in childbirth and be ruled by her husband. Adam would sweat and work hard all the days of his life with fewer results. And they would both return to dust. (See vv. 16-19.) If that wasn't enough, God sent them out of the garden of Eden, a place of peace, purpose, and provision . . . *but He didn't take back the breath of life.* That light was still within them.

What does this have to do with letting go of your private pain? Both Adam and Eve suffered painful losses. I'm sure they both had deep regrets. But God made sure to give them hope. He declared the Seed of the woman—Jesus Christ—would have victory over the serpent's seed. Although God disciplined Adam and Eve, He also made sure they knew that they were still in a posture of victory over the enemy (the serpent). They could move forward after their loss and still lead positive, productive lives. So can you.

I'll say it again: The end depends upon the beginning. Perhaps, like me, you have suffered the loss of a loved one. Maybe you've lost your job or your health or have gone through a difficult divorce. No matter what you may have lost, there is still life within you. God made sure of that in the beginning. The promise of life and light is as real now as it was then. You can come all the way through the grief process and have hope for better, brighter tomorrows.

HOLD ON TO YOUR TREASURE

So hold your focus, hold on to your faith in Christ, as we move forward. Cherish the treasure He's given you.

Society views treasure as accumulated wealth or valuable resources, like gold, precious stones, and so on. These treasures can be temporary. You can also treasure someone or something that's precious to you, like a loved one, your health, a family heirloom, or even knowledge you've acquired. But there will be times when, for one reason or another, a loved one can't be there for you. An issue could come up with your health or finances. A family keepsake could be lost. Something you learn today could become obsolete in the not-too-distant future.

But the treasure inside of you—*the light of the knowledge of the glory of God in the face of Jesus Christ*—is eternal. It doesn't change or become obsolete. Jesus Christ is the same

yesterday, today, and forever (see Hebrews 13:8). His finished work on the cross is as valid today as it was when He
died and rose from the grave. *The devil can't ever take this
light away from you.* Why? Jesus has stripped him of his
authority and delivered you from the power of darkness.
(See Colossians 1:13-14; 2:13-15; Hebrews 2:14-15; and
Revelation 1:18.)

You can do all things through Christ who strengthens you!
The light of Jesus shines within you . . . on your best days
and in your darkest hours. Pain and grief can't extinguish His
light. But if you pull away from God in the darkness, then
you can give up what He has freely given you. Don't let the
enemy steal your treasure. Keep your focus on God and
you'll come through private pain into healing and victory.

Here's a handy tip from my booklet, *30 Minutes in Prayer*:
A little dab will do you. What does this mean? As I said in
my booklet, "You can start right where you are and just do
'a little'; then you can build from there . . . As you believe
God, keep coming to Him, and faithfully do what He
instructs you to do, He'll do what only He can do in your
life. Your part is to believe God, come to Him, and obey. His
part is to order your steps, reshape your life and lead you
into your divine destiny."[2]

With this in mind, here's a nugget of wisdom to light your
day: *Keep a song in your heart.* In fact, I'd like to suggest the
perfect one: "This Little Light of Mine" by Harry Dixon
Loes. I'm sure you've heard of this popular gospel song. You

may even know the melody by heart. Here are some of the lyrics to help keep you focused on the promise:

> This little light of mine, I'm gonna let it shine . . .
> Jesus gave me the light, I'm gonna let it shine . . .
> Don't let the Satan blow it out, I'm gonna let it shine . . .
> Let it shine. Let it shine. Let it shine.

Just thinking about this simple message lifts my spirit and stirs my faith. How about you?

Here's another promising thought: "He who has begun a good work in you will complete it until the day of Jesus Christ" (Philippians 1:6). Believe it! Let it shine in your heart. Jesus is the *author* and *finisher* of your faith (see Hebrews 12:2). From the moment He gave you eternal life, Jesus was fully committed to be with you, *and in you*, always. He'll walk with you every step of the way as you come through the grief process.

I know from personal experience there is no pain so severe that God can't heal you. There is no loss so deep that He can't restore you. (I'll be sharing some of my story with you starting in the next chapter.) Jesus' light within you overcomes darkness. It dries your tears, heals your hurts, and strengthens you to finish the course.

Just hold on to your faith. *Believe Him, come to Him*, and *obey Him* as you deal with private pain. The process of letting go is much easier with the Lord than without Him. And remember, a little dab will do you. Do what you can and the

Lord will do what only He can do. Hope, healing, and victory are yours in Jesus Christ.

STAY FOCUSED ON THE LIGHT

Now that we've examined our treasure and focused on God's promises, it's time to move forward. It's always best to get off to a strong start, don't you agree? Because again, the end depends upon the beginning.

Here's a final tip: *Bookmark this chapter.* Come back to it whenever your faith is challenged. That way, you'll stay focused on the light—not the light at the end of the tunnel— the light, the treasure, within you . . . and it will *shine, shine, shine.* Let me pray for you as I close.

Father God, we enter Your presence with thanksgiving and praise. You are King of kings, Lord of lords, and Master of the universe. You are Abba, our Father in heaven. Thank You for speaking light into darkness and for giving us the eternal promise that we can overcome the enemy in Jesus Christ. You are the light of life within us: a treasure in our earthen vessels. We could never repay You for the love You have freely bestowed upon us, so we give You our whole hearts and lives. We hold on to faith in You, Lord. Let Your eternal light shine brightly within us. I ask that just as You have delivered us from the power of darkness, that You would give my friend who is reading this book hope and strength to expose, confront, and let go of private pain. Help my friend to focus on You, keep coming to You in prayer, and obediently follow You during each step of the grief process. Thank You for giving hope and peace as only You can do and for bringing complete healing and restoration. We thank You as we move forward that Your Word will never pass away and that You always keep Your promises. Our hope is in You, Father God . . . for Yours is the kingdom, the power, and the glory forever. In the priceless name of Jesus we pray. Amen.

FAITH CHECK

Finally, before you start reading the next chapter, I want to make sure we're on solid footing. Are you confident of your salvation? Do you have any reason to doubt that you have truly received Jesus Christ as your Savior and Lord? If you answered no and yes, then bow your heart before the Lord with me and say the following prayer:

Dear Lord Jesus, I believe You are the Son of God and that You died and rose from the dead for my sin. Come into my heart. Forgive me, Lord. Fill me with Your life. Thank You for loving me, saving me from the power of darkness, and restoring me to the Father. I receive You with my whole heart and will follow You for the rest of my life. In Your name I pray. Amen.

Perhaps you're saved, but you have walked away from the Lord. There is no better time than the present to get things right with Him. Say this prayer with me:

> *Dear Lord Jesus, I come into Your presence giving You praise. Forgive me for walking away from You, Lord. I'm sorry for taking my focus off of You and doing what seemed right in my own eyes. I confess and renounce my sins. [Take a few moments to confess and renounce each one and give it to the Lord.] Thank You, Lord, that Your Word promises if I confess my sins You will forgive me of my sins and cleanse me from all unrighteousness. Create in me a clean heart and renew a right spirit within me. Restore the joy of my salvation and my first love for You. Lord, I ask You to give me hearing ears and an obedient heart. Stir my soul so I thirst for Your presence like a deer pants for water. Re-ignite the fire of holy passion in me. I will follow You from this day forward, Lord. Thank You for loving, forgiving, and restoring me. In Your name I pray. Amen.*

Praise the Lord! Whether you prayed either of those prayers or are fully confident of your salvation and intimacy with the Lord, we're ready to take the next step. You don't have to be afraid of the dark. You're a child of God. You have a priceless treasure within you—the light of eternal life.

CHAPTER 2

EXPOSING PRIVATE PAIN
The Light Shines in Darkness

O God, listen to my cry! Hear my prayer!
From the ends of the earth,
I cry to you for help when my heart is overwhelmed.
Lead me to the towering rock of safety,
for you are my safe refuge,
a fortress where my enemies cannot reach me.
Let me live forever in your sanctuary,
safe beneath the shelter of your wings!
PSALM 61:1-4 (NLT)

The weekend of March 19, 2011, marked the two-year anniversary of losing my first son, Larry Lawrence Brandon, III. As I went about my activities, thoughts of my son kept cycling through my mind. Each time I experienced a memory and the sharp sting of pain that came afterward, I prayed silently and kept moving forward. Then on Sunday, when I hosted the "I Am My Faith" radio show before our morning church service, it became evident God was up to something. My spirit was stirring. I felt strongly led to share more about what I had gone through. As I obeyed God and opened up about my private pain, I was amazed at the results.

Let me start from the beginning in 2009 so you can see how God transforms private pain into public victory. My son's death was totally unexpected; he was killed in a random shooting in Fairfield, California. The day it happened I was on my way to a meeting and a photo shoot when I received a text message: "Larry, Little Larry is dead."

I was stunned. I couldn't believe my eyes. What could have possibly happened? This couldn't be real. I took a deep breath and called my mother to confirm it. Up to this point, though I was in shock about receiving the message, I was actually handling myself pretty well. Then I heard her voice: "Hey baby . . . " From her tone and demeanor, I knew it was real. There's a certain way she says things when something has gone wrong.

She hadn't even finished her sentence when I said, "My son is dead." Sadly, she said yes, and then started telling me what had happened. At that point, I lost it emotionally. I had to take some quiet time alone. I said, "Momma, pray for me," and told her I would call her back.

The sting of my son's loss was intense. When I hung up the phone, a feeling of grief I had never experienced in my life overcame me. So many intense emotions set in. I didn't want to speak to anyone. I couldn't even pray.

A little while later, after gathering myself, I called her back and got some more information. Interestingly, though the reality of my son's death was sinking in, I was still in a state of disbelief. You don't want to believe someone you love is gone, especially under such sudden and tragic circumstances.

It came to me that I still had an appointment coming up at the church, so I gathered myself as best I could. I said, "Lord, I need You to help me. I'm Your son, and I'm on assignment, but I'm human." Of course, God was well aware of that. He had been with me every minute since I received the terrible news. God isn't put off by our pain. His strength is made perfect in our weaknesses (see 2 Corinthians 12:9). The more you need Him, the more He is there.

I went on to the church and took care of the remaining business, not saying a word about what had happened. Nobody knew what was going on.

Before I left the office I called my wife, Wanda, told her what had happened, and asked her to gather the children. I wanted all of us to be together when I told them about Larry. I also asked her not to answer the phone; I knew that soon everybody would be calling to console us. "Just sit still until I get there," I said.

My drive home was a long journey. As I took the familiar

streets and turns, my emotions were all over the place. I was struggling . . . but I knew by the time I got home I needed to be strong for my family. When I got to the house, I composed myself and walked in. I went to my family, sat among them, and shared what had happened to Larry. Understandably, they were shocked and extremely upset to hear what had taken place and that he was no longer with us.

I gave them time to release their emotions. Then something happened that touched me deeply. My daughter came to me, hugged me, and said, "Daddy, are you okay?" I broke down again . . . because my baby was comforting me. Once again, I had to take some time alone. I asked them to gather themselves and told them I'd be back soon. Then I left the house to take another "journey" and come to terms with my own grief.

This time, as I pondered what had happened to my son, I became angry . . . first of all, with God. I said to the Lord, "Now, how can I serve You and minister to so many people, and have something like this happen to me? This was my son. I've been ministering Your Word and pushing people to their next level; helping their children and prophesying into their lives. I've been pouring out my heart for ministry, and my son, my flesh and blood, my namesake, Larry Lawrence Brandon, III, has been ripped out of my life."

I had to admit: Not only was I angry at God, I was livid with anyone who had had anything at all to do with my son's untimely death. I even had thoughts of avenging his death.

I thank God for His tender mercies and for the light of Jesus in my soul. As I continued to cry out before Him, He spoke to my spirit. A scripture passage came to my heart . . . Psalm 61:1-4, which is on the first page of this chapter. As I remembered these words, God strengthened me:

> O God, listen to my cry!
> Hear my prayer!
> From the ends of the earth,
> I cry to you for help
> when my heart is overwhelmed.
> Lead me to the towering rock of safety,
> for you are my safe refuge,
> a fortress where my enemies cannot reach me.
> Let me live forever in your sanctuary,
> safe beneath the shelter of your wings!

The Lord is a refuge of hope, strength, and peace in our time of need. He is a "safe place" for us to hide when we're broken and at the end of ourselves. *Have you experienced His tender, healing touch in your darkest hour?* I certainly hope so. Nothing in this world can compare to it. When God reminds you of His Word and comforts you, it goes to the depths of your soul. It soothes your pain and gives you indescribable peace. It gives you hope when everything around you tells you that all hope is gone.

That psalm was so calming to me. Not only did it confirm the cry of my heart, it also reminded me that God understood my pain. He would keep me safe under the shelter of His wings as I walked through this painful process. That night I went home comforted by the Lord. I said, "All right, Lord. You've helped me all these years; You can help me through this as well."

GOD STANDS BY HIS WORD

Hebrews 4:12 in the *Amplified Bible* says: "For the Word that God speaks is alive and full of power [making it active, operative, energizing, and effective]; it is sharper than any two-edged sword, penetrating to the dividing line of the breath of life (soul) and [the immortal] spirit, and of joints and marrow [of the deepest parts of our nature], exposing and sifting and analyzing and judging the very thoughts and purposes of the heart."

A dear friend of ours once shared with me about her private pain when her mother passed away. Her testimony is also proof of the power of God's Word. This friend's mother had been ill for many years. She had gone through a painful divorce and had lived a difficult life afterward. Years later things finally started taking a turn for the better. Everything was coming full circle, and her mother was settled and happy. Then one day our friend received a phone call from her stepfather.

"How's everybody doing?" she asked. "Not well," he said. "When I came home today your mother was dead on the living room floor . . . "

She froze. "What?" She couldn't believe what she had just heard. She dropped to the floor and listened numbly while he told her what had happened. Then she went into a room by herself and sat in silence. A little while later, the Holy Spirit spoke in her heart, "They are going to ask you to sing . . . " Within thirty minutes, one of her sisters called and asked if she could sing at the funeral.

She didn't know how she could possibly do it but said yes anyway. She felt that because the Lord had prepared her for this call, and He didn't tell her not to do it, she should trust Him and honor her mother before they laid her to rest. "Just have somebody ready in case I can't make it through the song," she said.

Less than a week later, the family was gathered at their mother's home, waiting for the limousines to arrive. She had been doing pretty well up to that point; it helped to be among family. When she went to stand at the front screen door and watched the limousines pull up, a tidal wave of grief came up within her. She felt herself losing composure. Then she heard the Holy Spirit say, "Read the Word."

She quickly got her Bible, opened it, and started reading. It didn't matter to her what book of the Bible or verse she turned to. She focused her eyes on a page and started reading. She needed God . . . right then. As she read, the pain began to subside. So she continued to read as they got into the limousines. She read while her siblings sat together in the car and wept. Then hope rose up within her. Suddenly, she looked up and heard herself saying, "Mom is in a better place now. She's young, beautiful, and healthy . . . " As she continued, she knew they probably thought she was crazy; but she couldn't deny the joy she felt sharing her faith.

When the limousines pulled up to the church, grief welled up within her again. She flipped the Bible open and started to read. She kept it open while she walked into the building, saw her mother's coffin up front, and then continued reading when she sat down. Only the Lord could give her the strength to stand at the podium over her mother's body and sing "Amazing Grace."

When she was called up to the platform, she took the Bible with her. Then she set it on the podium, opened it, laid her hand on the pages, and sang,

> Amazing grace! How sweet the sound
> that saved a wretch like me!
> I once was lost, but now am found;
> was blind, but now I see.

She had planned to sing the first and last verses.

An unbelievable sense of peace filled our friend as she sang. She felt strength rising inside of her. And to her amazement, she didn't miss a note. She got stronger and stronger, both vocally and emotionally, as she continued the song. Instead of stopping after two verses, she added a verse of her own at the end that consisted of two simple, yet powerful, words: "Praise God, praise God, praise God, praise God . . . "

To this day our friend can't find words to fully explain what she experienced that day. She had an encounter with the Lord in her darkest hour, and He overflowed her with life. She trusted Him, did what she was able to do, and then God did what only He could do.

She didn't realize it then, but the invitation to sing at her mother's funeral was part of her healing process. Not only did God strengthen her through His Word, He also made sure she had a song in her heart. Although she was grieving the sudden loss of her mother, she trusted God and let her treasure, the light of Jesus, shine brilliantly in the darkness. It lifted her countenance and ministered life to everyone in that place.

If you are facing a mountain of grief, let me encourage you again: *A little dab will do you.* Believe God, come to Him, and obey Him. He'll do the rest. God loves you. He won't leave you in the dark. If you'll trust Him, even when it hurts, you'll discover what I've learned time and again since I asked Jesus to come into my heart. The more you need Him, the more He is there.

GOD EXPOSES PAIN AND GRIEF

Hebrews 4:13 (AMP) says: "And not a creature exists that is concealed from His sight, but all things are open and exposed, naked and defenseless to the eyes of Him with Whom we have to do." God knows our pain. At times (even when we're not aware of it), He intervenes and prevents us from having painful experiences. At other times, He comes to us when we're hurting and shines a light in our soul. He exposes our private pain so we can deal with it.

On Saturday, March 19, 2011, the memory of my son's death two years before brought some issues back to the surface. Each time I experienced a painful memory, I prayed and kept going about my day. I was still keeping my grief private, reasoning to myself that I needed to be strong for my family, my congregation, and others. However, the Lord reminded me that day that I had told Him I wanted to show His people how to grieve. He answered that prayer sooner than I thought.

Psalm 34:17-18 says, "The righteous cry out, and the Lord hears, and delivers them out of all their troubles. The Lord is near to those who have a broken heart, and saves such as have a contrite spirit." God cares about His people. He responds when we cry out to Him.

That Sunday morning as I went to the Lord in prayer, He shined a light in my soul. I knew what I had to do. When the "I Am My Faith" radio show went on the air, I announced that the subject of the day was "Private Pain." During that program, a man called in and began to share about something painful he had gone through. I felt his grief and started sharing some of the things I had been challenged with personally. He seemed liberated by my testimony, so I continued in the flow.

Then a lady called in who had lost her mother thirty years before and was still suffering. She said until I opened the mic that day, she hadn't been able to release her pain. Then others began to call in and thank us for sharing. Each of them had painful issues they needed to release. One by one, they shared their stories and asked me to pray with them. God was moving powerfully and giving people breakthroughs.

This fueled my fire. By the time I walked into the sanctuary to minister the Word of the Lord in the morning service, I was primed and ready. I could feel His presence in the room. And I sensed the needs of the people. When I shared the message, I was as transparent as I had been on the radio program. I opened up about things I had been dealing with since the death of my son and how I was able to keep moving forward. The power of God kept flowing.

As I released my private pain, people literally started crying out, and by the time I opened the altar for ministry, people were popping up all over the room. They were so drunk with the Word that they lost all inhibition and came running to the front of the church. And I noticed a lot of men were getting up first, as if they didn't care who saw them.

I was overwhelmed. The altar was jam-packed. I would say men represented at least 70 percent of the people who had come forward. There they were, all lined up, openly releasing their grief. It is more common for women to come forward for prayer. But for a man to come forward for help is major; we are more prideful than women. Think about it. A woman will go to the doctor in a minute to get checked out; most men have to feel like they're almost dying before getting medical help. It amazed me that so many men were responding to the Lord and openly expressing their private pain.

That day was explosive. And it was most liberating for me because I had bottled up my grief and not spoken about it for two long years. I wasn't comfortable sharing my private pain with others. As a leader, I felt that I shouldn't burden them with my struggle. But that day when I released my private pain, I felt so refreshed. I found healing when God tapped my treasure and I let my light shine in the darkness for His glory.

From that point on, God began to minister to me on a new level. The healing process had truly begun . . . in me and in the lives of many others who cried out to the Lord for help.

FAITH CHECK

Let me close this chapter with a word of advice: When you hold on to your pain, you're letting go of your faith in that area. I have learned this lesson well. But as you hold on to your faith in God, you let go of the pain that holds you in darkness. You have eternal treasure, the light of life, within you. Sometimes letting it shine in the dark can be very different than you think . . . but it is powerfully productive.

The American writer, Washington Irving, once said: "There is a sacredness in tears. They are not the mark of weakness, but of power. They speak more eloquently than ten thousand tongues. They are messengers of overwhelming grief . . . and unspeakable love."[1] When you cry out to the Lord, His strength is made perfect in your weakness. So don't be afraid of the dark. And don't try to escape your tears. They can release light and life to everyone around you.

What is your private pain? Have you been holding it in, not wanting to expose it to others? If so, why? Don't answer too quickly. Let's pause and bow our hearts before the Lord in prayer:

> *Dear Lord Jesus, we come into Your presence with thanksgiving. Thank You for giving us life and light. You are our "safe refuge" when our hearts are overwhelmed, an ever-present help in our time of need. Hide us under the shelter of Your wings and expose our private pain. Bring everything to mind that we need to let go of so the healing process can begin. We submit ourselves to You, Lord. Thank You for the treasure You have placed within us, because Your light overcomes darkness. In Your name we pray. Amen.*

Now take some time to reflect, and then answer the questions as openly and honestly as you can. Write your thoughts in a journal if you'd like. Then submit your private pain to the Lord. Settle it in your heart that when God calls upon you to shine in the darkness you will trust Him and obey.

CHAPTER 3

LET'S KEEP IT REAL

Don't Hide Your Treasure

*Also He said to them, "Is a lamp brought to be put
under a basket or under a bed? Is it not to be set on a
lampstand? For there is nothing hidden which will not be
revealed, nor has anything been kept secret but that it should
come to light. If anyone has ears to hear, let him hear."*

MARK 4:21-23

Seeing how God exposed and delivered hundreds of
people from private pain in our Sunday service that day
was a tipping point for me. Although I was blessed we had
experienced this sovereign move of God, I realized that people don't generally feel comfortable sharing their problems in

church. Too often, they feel like they have to wear a public mask. This is the opposite of what Jesus wants. He puts light within us to expose darkness, not to conceal it.

So what makes us hide our treasure? Why do we tend to put our "lamp" underneath our pain so darkness isn't exposed? No matter how awkward or difficult it seems to be, we need to start by taking off our masks and admitting we have a problem. Hiding our pain freezes our progress. If we want to come all the way through the grieving process, we need to take down the façade that tells everyone around us we are picture-perfect.

Let's take down some walls, shall we? I'll start with the big-picture view. From my standpoint as an overseer of churches and a ministry leader, I believe more people would share their pain if the environment in church was conducive. I say this very soberly: often, the settings in churches don't help people feel comfortable releasing their private pain. I've heard it said that it's easier to talk to a sinner than it is to talk to a saint . . . because sinners won't judge you but saints will. I believe we tend to be judgmental because we haven't been keeping it real.

First of all, when visiting a church, you immediately become aware of how people act and the way things are done. You get an initial feel for how you'd fit in. Chances are you felt right at home when you walked into the church you now attend. You have probably also visited churches where you felt like you needed to button up your jacket and put on your best behavior. That type of environment doesn't put you at ease. It doesn't facilitate you feeling comfortable just being yourself.

Don't get me wrong. It's important to make sure everything is in order for services. But this should include putting things in place so that everyone—visitors and members—feel welcomed and accepted. Are the staff, leaders, and workers comfortable enough in their own skin to maintain decorum while being real? This is important, because people can see through pretense . . . and they expect a higher standard of behavior in church than in the world.

While we worship and serve God in church, whether we're in church leadership or not, we need to take our guard down enough to show our humanity. If not, we're hiding our treasure.

I mean no disrespect to anyone, but I believe another reason people become uncomfortable in church is many of us tend to take the "cookie cutter" approach to ministry. Trying to deal with everyone the same way or using the same method to address every issue is counterproductive. Something that works in one situation may not work in another, no matter how similar they may be.

We talk in "Christianese" and, all too often, don't back up our words with faith-filled action. Our culture is filled with so much "church language" that when people hear it, they often don't believe it. The power that was once behind our words is no longer there because we use them too loosely. We treat ourselves so casually that if someone makes a statement that sounds "too churchy," we take it for granted.

People's lives are too important to have a one-size-fits-all mentality. Among other things, there are those who have psychiatric and physical illnesses who need to be directed properly. How many people would be alive and well today if someone had directed them saying, "Go seek medical attention, and we'll believe God for healing," instead of saying, "You'll be all right; the Lord will make a way"?

We simply need to do better. We need to be more mindful to watch while we pray, listen while we interact, and *follow-up* while we manage our daily schedules.

As Christians we are a spiritual people, but we need to be practical enough to see and respond to everyday needs and issues. Ministry is about worshiping God and loving people. So we need to be relatable: to God and to each other. Well-known author and motivational speaker John Maxwell said, "People do not care how much you know until they know how much you care."[1] I've found this is absolutely true. Being overly spiritual and out-of-touch makes people put up guards and take out masks faster than any minister would like to admit. That being the case, we need to trust God and do whatever we can to change the atmosphere in our churches.

When I remember Psalm 61:1-4, it not only reminds me that God is a "safe place" to hide when our hearts are overwhelmed, it also challenges me to make our church a house of refuge for all who come to worship. If you've ever felt put off because the environment at church made you feel uncomfortable, don't give up hope. Trust God, pray, and be willing to open up. He might even use your testimony to bring a breakthrough.

TAKE OFF YOUR "PUBLIC MASK"

God is working in all of us—from the pulpit to the pew— to keep it real. Let's focus on a few other ways believers tend to hide our treasure and put on a "public mask." After all, not feeling comfortable to share our private pain in church isn't always the result of a failure in leadership. Often, people also have personal values and issues that keep them from being transparent.

I have found the general attitude tends to be: "I have 2.5 children, a house and two cars, and everybody's fine." While it may be generally true that many adults have children, a mortgage, and necessary transportation, everything isn't always all right. When things aren't going well, we need to stop being so superficial about our pain. We need to take off our public mask and cry out to God. Sometimes He chooses to move sovereignly in a corporate setting, like during a Sunday worship service. So if you can't open up in front of your brothers and sisters in Christ, you could miss a divine opportunity to be healed and delivered.

Why do people have problems letting down their guards in church? In many households (I know in my household growing up), children are taught what goes on in the house stays in the house. When you grow up with that belief, you carry that personal value into the culture, which extends into the church.

Has this been your experience? Do you feel it's wrong to open up about your private pain? It's time to expose the real issue. If that is your background, even if you haven't given much thought to it, it could be affecting how you relate to others. It could be causing you to put up walls of protection that keep anyone from getting too close.

For example, have you ever regularly sat next to someone in church, maybe even gone out to eat afterward, believing he or she is the picture of health, only to find out later that person has heart disease or some other major health issue? If so, you were probably surprised when you found out. You might have wondered why that person didn't openly say, "The reason I'm not eating certain foods is because I'm trying to take care of my health. I have this issue . . . " It's easy to mask our pain.

Now don't get me wrong; there's definitely a place for discretion concerning our personal lives. But we have to get better at letting down our guards—and taking down our walls—in the family of God. Think about it. More often than not, Jesus was in the midst of a lot of people when He healed the sick. Often, those who wanted to be healed approached

Him in a crowd. They didn't let anything hold them back from releasing their private pain. You can't hide your treasure, stay behind a protective façade, and be restored. Even though you may have been raised to keep everything private, it's just not God's way of doing things.

God wants you to be whole: spiritually, physically, financially, and emotionally. So when you come to Him, including when you attend church, think holistically. The needs you have behind the walls of your own home are just as valid and relevant in God's house. Jesus can touch, heal, and restore you if you're willing to come out of the dark.

GET RID OF FALSE "IMAGES"

Another reason people put on public masks is they build images of themselves they don't want to shatter. For example, if you're a big giver in your church, you may be reluctant to go there for help if you're having financial problems. If you're a leader and known as one of the elites, you may avoid turning to the church for help when you have a family issue—because you've built a strong image. That's a problem. Second Corinthians 10:3-5 (KJV) says:

> For though we walk in the flesh, we do not war after the flesh: (for the weapons of our warfare are not carnal but mighty through God to the pulling down of strong holds;)

casting down imaginations, and every high thing *that exalt-eth itself against the knowledge of God, and bringing into captivity every thought to the obedience of Christ"* [emphasis mine].

In other words, though we walk in human flesh, we're not supposed to contend in natural ways, struggling to obtain or maintain what we think God wants or approves of. But He can give us supernatural power to pull down "strong holds" and "imaginations" in our own minds, so we will keep our eyes on Him and off our own "images."

Let me put it this way. We can believe God, attend church, and do all the things that demonstrate a life of faith. But if we take our eyes off of God, we can build images (strongholds) in our minds about the "great things" we've done. That's when we let go of faith in those areas. Soon after, we start putting on public masks to protect our image and conceal our private pain. It's a vicious cycle.

Let's take a moment to remember the treasure within us. Second Corinthians 4:6-7 says:

For it is the God who commanded light to shine out of darkness, who has shone in our hearts to give *the light of the knowledge of the glory of God in the face of Jesus Christ*. But we have this treasure in earthen vessels, that the excellence of the power may be of God and not of us [emphasis mine].

Do you see how both passages from Second Corinthians relate? *We have to keep our eyes on Jesus to keep it real: with Him and with each other.* The devil, the enemy of our souls, is skilled at making us think our images are our treasure. This couldn't be farther from the truth. No matter what we have or haven't accomplished, we need to keep our eyes on the Lord—because where our treasure is, our hearts will be also (see Matthew 6:21).

The images we allow to form in our minds can hurt us. In fact, they often become gods . . . and the Lord has made it very plain we are not to put other gods before Him. (See Exodus 20:1-6 and 1 John 5:18-21.)

The enemy wants you to think that you can't tell anyone when you're struggling. He'll use childhood values, cultural influences, strongholds in your mind—and anything else he can muster—against you. He wants you to hold on to private pain in an attempt to save face and avoid losing stature and respect. This is an age-old spiritual warfare tactic. Hear me: You can't take on this battle alone. You need to hold on to your faith in God and stand in agreement with other believers.

If you're a leader in the church and are suffering a loss in any area of your life, don't hide your pain. Don't think, *If I let people know, they may take away my responsibilities for a season and I'll be embarrassed.* Depending on the severity of your situation, it might be good to take some time and come to terms with your grief. God wants you to be whole.

I'm sure you've heard the saying that healthy people help people, but hurting people hurt people. As believers and servants of the Lord, we can't let images put us in the position where we could potentially be hurting people, thinking we're helping them. That's also an age-old trick of the enemy.

Whether or not you're a leader in the church, it's vitally important for you to expose your pain. I believe things come along to remind the saints that we're still human. Seek the Lord in the Word and in prayer. Get godly counsel and guidance. Cry out to God, even if it's during a church service. This will give you assurance you're going to make it all the way through to healing and victory, and help you deal with your pain as you go through the process.

There is a lot of risk involved in being transparent, but it's important to run the risk. I would rather take the risk and walk in divine healing, than to hold on to my pain and potentially self-destruct. This happens too often in the church. People are wearing public masks and self-destructing because they haven't shared their challenges—financial, physical, emotional, or spiritual—with the Lord or anyone else.

The devil plays mind games. We have to deal with our images. We have to acknowledge that although we are sons and daughters of God, we are also human. Walking in the darkness shining the light of Jesus is a daily war. We have to put on the whole armor of God and fight the good fight of faith to stand against the wiles of the devil. (See Ephesians 6:11-18 and 1 Timothy 6:12.)

I believe the church is a spiritual hospital—we're all sick, trying to get well. There are times God exposes our pain because He wants to heal it. He'll allow certain things to happen so we'll press the reset button and cry out to Him.

It's just like having the flu. If you don't go to see a doctor, you may get over it, but the bug will still be in your body. Unless you get medical advice and take antibiotics, you'll likely have a recurrence, and then your condition could turn into pneumonia. On the same note, if you don't deal with private pain properly and release it, it can come back on you, and it will be worse. The devil will play with your mind and bring images to you over and over again. If you put on a public mask and pretend your pain doesn't exist, it can become insurmountable.

We must keep it real. We need to be willing to say, "Hey, I have issues. Pray with me." Don't let the enemy (in-a-me) keep you bound up with private pain. Your issues aren't going anywhere unless you release them—*because they're real*. Whatever struggles you mask follow you wherever you go, including when you go to the house of God. The church is full of people who are suffering from private pain.

I'm not saying to go around telling all of your business, because some people are just nosey busybodies. Just help yourself out a little. Let go of images, open up, and release some of those pesky issues. You never know who may be in the congregation that God has assigned to minister to you and personally walk alongside you during tough times. You also never know whose life you're going to touch when you open up and share your testimony. That's why the enemy wants you to put on a public mask and keep everything to yourself. He's trying to steal healing and deliverance from God's people.

BEWARE OF DELILAH

The story of Samson and Delilah in Judges 16 is a perfect example. The Bible says Samson had "great strength." By the time he met Delilah he was a judge in Israel, so he had established a solid image. But Samson was suffering from private pain. How do I know this? Judges 14:1-20 tells about the events that unfolded when Samson found a woman in a city named Timnah whom he wanted to marry, but she was a Philistine—Israel's enemy that ruled over them.

Of course, Samson's parents didn't agree he should marry her, but the text says it was God's will for him to love her because the Lord was " . . . seeking an occasion to move against the Philistines" (v. 4). So, carrying the pain of his parents objecting to his marriage, Samson went through the process of marrying her anyway.

As it turned out, this woman for whom he would do anything in the world betrayed him to her people (you can read the story for details). After everything played out, unbeknownst to Samson, her father gave her to the man who had been Samson's best man. Then when Samson went back to get her, more events unfolded that led to the Philistines killing both her and her father in a fire (15:1-6).

The next woman Samson fell in love with was Delilah. Up to this point, the Philistines had both heard of and experienced Samson's amazing strength. He had killed a lion with his bare hands (14:5-6); he had killed thirty men in Ashkelon (14:19), and he had killed a thousand men in Lehi with the jawbone of a donkey (15:14-17). Yet, somehow, getting even with his enemies didn't satisfy his grief.

After being betrayed by the first woman he had ever loved, Samson didn't know who to believe or how to deal with his pain. But he had already fallen for this alluring Philistine woman. Delilah, on the other hand, had been bribed to find out the source of Samson's great strength. So she immediately started pressing him to tell her.

It took a little time for Samson to trust her, but when he told her he had been devoted to God from birth and for that reason his hair had never been cut, she turned on him. She lulled him to sleep, called someone to cut his hair, had him bound, and then called for the lords of the Philistines. When Samson woke up, it was too late. He no longer had the strength to escape and fight. So they captured him, put out his eyes, and took him to prison in Gaza (16:1-21).

It's hard to understand how such a strong man could become so weak. But like Samson, we often don't want to display our weakness; we want to be known for our strength.

This is especially true for leaders. There are times when well-meaning people hype us up, so we feel we can't be transparent and show our weaknesses. Everybody believes in us. Hear me: Trust God and be willing to show your humanity. If you're focused on your own images, people can push you over the top.

Samson hadn't really dealt with his private pain. As a result, he became vulnerable to Israel's enemy. But thankfully, that's not the end of the story. Verse 22 says the hair of his head began to grow again. To make a long story short, he later called out to the Lord at a strategic moment and God strengthened him to take down more Philistines in his death than he had during his life (vv. 23-30).

I want you to notice: Samson cried out to God three times in the text. He cried out for water after killing the thousand men in Lehi (Judges 15:18). He called to the Lord in Gaza for strength to take vengeance on the Philistines (16:28). Then in his last words, Samson cried out to God, "Let me die with the Philistines!" (16:30). Each time Samson cried out to God, He responded. If only Samson had been more focused on that earlier in his grief process, his story might have ended differently.

Also notice Samson had a conversation with Delilah about his strength, his anointing, and she used it against him. When you're dealing with private pain, never entertain the enemy. Release your images, give your pain to the Lord, and submit to godly counsel for agreement and guidance. Don't take matters into your own hands. The enemy is very subtle. He often comes to us in ways that appeal to our senses. But his intent is always to steal, kill, and destroy.

Everyone has a "Delilah," a person, place, or thing that can entice us to sin. Oftentimes, we reach out to the wrong person, place, or thing when we're feeling weak. Delilah will show up to soothe you when you're vulnerable. Delilah could be drugs, alcohol, or some other form of negative pain reliever. If you don't deal with private pain, you could end up reaching out for negative pain relief. Don't believe the lie of the enemy. This soothing substitute will prove to be detrimental.

When Samson entertained the enemy (Delilah), he lost his anointing. The moment he tried to shake himself free, he found out his strength (anointing) was no longer there. Sometimes we keep going through the motions, taking a pain reliever instead of dealing with our pain, and find the anointing has been lifted. We thought we were okay, but we weren't. Let me remind you: It's okay to admit when we're not okay. God can help us become whole again.

You see, Samson's situation with Delilah didn't happen overnight. She was very patient. Samson was suffering from a great deal of mental anguish due to the betrayal and death of his former wife. Just think of the grief he was probably experiencing. To make things worse, after he trusted Delilah (the second woman he trusted), he was blinded and thrown into prison.

But in Samson's darkest hour, God restored him. His hair grew back, his anointing returned, and he regained his strength. However, Samson's final request was to die with the Philistines. I personally think he didn't have to pray that prayer. Nothing is impossible with God. Samson could have killed the Philistines and lived on.

I think Samson's last words reveal he was depressed. I believe though Samson was still thankful to God for anointing him, he no longer felt worthy to live . . . so he prayed to die with those who had harmed him. *I urge you: No matter what you're going through, don't hold on to private pain and let go of the life, the treasure, within you.* Putting on a public mask could ultimately lead to disaster. Cry out to God for healing and live on! Let your light shine in the darkness.

I thank God for allowing Samson to become an example for us. He was very strong, yet he was weak. We need to take note of this. If we're not careful, our strength can become our weakness. Sometimes we think we're so strong that we don't need the Lord. We think that we can handle our own situations and pain. Then when a challenge arises that taps our weakness, we discover our own strength isn't enough.

Releasing private pain can help you grow your hair back and regain sight and strength, so you can move forward and complete your God-given assignment. So be transparent and keep it real: at home, at work, and especially in church. Let go of your images and let your light shine, shine, shine. Your healing process can begin . . . but it won't start until you're not afraid to admit you're hurting: until you take off your public mask.

FAITH CHECK

There is an old Turkish Proverb that says: "He that conceals his grief finds no remedy for it."[2] If you've ever covered up grief, you know it doesn't go away on its own. You have to expose it to deal with it proactively. If you hide your grief, it can spin out of control and you won't know what hit you. Take a lesson from Jesus. He was a master at keeping it real. When people came to Him wearing masks He exposed the truth. And when He was sad, He cried—even if He was in a crowd (John 11:33-35).

Jesus also said everything that is kept secret will be revealed (Mark 4:22). Knowing this, it's much better to take off our own public masks and deal with private pain than to be caught off guard by the schemes of the enemy. Jesus heals our pain; the enemy exploits it.

Now take some time to consider and answer the following questions. I encourage you to write your thoughts in a journal. Not only will this help you to pray as you work through the process, you'll also be able to look back when you've come all the way through and give God the glory.

1. Were you taught growing up that everything that happens at home stays in the home? If so, has this kept you from opening up and being transparent with others? In what ways?
2. Have you built any images that you're afraid to tear down? What are they? List them in your mind and on paper. Make each one a matter of prayer, and be willing to do things differently the next time God presents an opportunity to take off your public mask.

Let's close in prayer.

Dear Lord Jesus, You are the light of the world that exposes and eliminates darkness. Help us receive Your light every day and in every situation. Lord, when we're hurting, help us come to You and be transparent with others. Reveal the secret areas that have caused us to put on public masks and hide our private pain. Help us keep it real, Lord, especially when we're in Your house, so we can be healed and delivered. We will obey You, Jesus. Thank You for working in us, both to will and do Your good pleasure. In Your great name we pray. Amen.

CHAPTER 4

WHEN WAITING GETS TOUGH

Real Treasure Endures!

Hope deferred makes the heart sick,
But when the desire comes, it is a tree of life

PROVERBS 13:12

During the altar call on the day I shared my private pain, someone came forward who was having severe financial issues. That person had planned to buy life insurance and do something drastic so the family could collect the funds. I thank God the mask came off, walls came down, and healing was released because the fate of an entire family was hanging in the balance. There were a number of other testimonies we heard from people with grief-stricken hearts, because it had looked like their promise would never come to pass.

When private pain goes unchecked, especially for extended periods of time, it can begin to run amuck. Out of hope and weary of waiting, we can let go of faith, take matters into our own hands, and then end up with bigger problems. *We have to remember: Real treasure endures.* James 1:17 (NLT) says: "Whatever is good and perfect comes down to us from God our Father, who created all the lights in the heavens. He never changes or casts a shifting shadow."

Have you been waiting for God to fulfill a promise in your life? I encourage you to wait on the Lord. Hold on to your faith. When God makes a promise, He keeps it. It's just a matter of time. The question is . . . do you trust His timing? I truly understand when people are overwhelmed with grief. When my son passed away, I experienced pain that I never thought could be possible. I couldn't imagine why God had allowed this to happen. In the normal scheme of things, we parents we expect our children to outlive us. Larry's passing just didn't make sense to me.

As I mentioned before, there were times I was tempted to take matters into my own hands. But if I had retaliated there would have been negative consequences that affected everyone in my sphere of influence—my family, friends, our congregation, the Full Gospel Baptist Church Fellowship (in which I'm a bishop), the various boards I'm a member of, and so on. If I had made a rash decision to "handle" my situation in anger, it would have caused widespread, detrimental results.

Had I let my grief get the best of me and allowed my actions to be unkind, I could have either gotten killed or arrested. Not to mention that the guilt I would have experienced afterward would certainly have made my private pain much worse.

There are consequences for our decisions: good or bad, happy or sad, wonderful or terrible. I was hurting deeply from my loss, but to act on my own against the counsel of God's Word would have complicated the situation. It would have assumed God wasn't willing or able to help me, and that couldn't be farther from the truth. And it would have set negative consequences in motion.

If you're hurting today, especially if you've been grieving for a long period of time, let me encourage you. Trust God. Go to Him in prayer. Cry out before Him. Get godly counsel and agreement in prayer. Do everything you can to be proactive and avoid making a rash emotional decision. *Guard your treasure—the light of the knowledge of the glory of God in the face of Jesus Christ.* No matter what changes come in your life, this eternal gift can never be taken away from you.

God is working "all things together" for your good—this includes frustrating times when you're in-between the present and the promise: the times when you want to give God a helping hand. Now don't get me wrong; God expects us to be productive. But He doesn't need our help to do what only He can do.

FAITH VERSUS PRESUMPTION

We've already seen from the life of Samson how unchecked private pain can birth bad decisions and untimely consequences. Let's take a look at another story that reveals how easily faith—even strong faith—can cross over into presumption. Genesis 12:1-3 tells us the Lord started Abram's journey with a great promise:

> Get out of your country, from your family and from your father's house, to a land that I will show you. I will make you a great nation; I will bless you and make your name great; and you shall be a blessing. I will bless those who bless you, and I will curse him who curses you; and in you all the families of the earth shall be blessed.

That's pretty powerful encouragement. In those words, God told Abram what He wanted him to do and gave him a vision for an incredible future. Then the process began. At seventy-five years of age Abram took his wife, his nephew, and all their possessions and left for the land of Canaan. As they were passing through Shechem, God spoke to Abram again and said: "To your descendants I will give this land." So Abram built an altar there. (See Genesis 12:4-7.)

When they came to Bethel, Abram built another altar "and called on the name of the LORD" (v. 8). In the Old Testament, building altars of sacrifice was a way to draw near to God and worship Him. So we see Abram honoring and acknowledging God during each step of his journey. In Genesis 15, God gave Abram a vision, saying:

> "Do not be afraid, Abram. I am your shield, your exceedingly great reward." But Abram said, "Lord GOD, what will You give me, seeing I go childless, and the heir of my house is Eliezer of Damascus? . . . Look, You have given me no offspring; indeed one born in my house is my heir!" And behold, the word of the Lord came to him saying, "This one shall not be your heir, but one who will come from your own body shall be your heir." Then He brought him outside and said, "Look now toward heaven, and count the stars if you are able to number them." And He said to him, "So shall your descendants be." And he believed in the LORD and He accounted it to him for righteousness. (vv. 1-6)

Let me pause here. When we read about Abram, who later became Abraham—a father of many nations—we need to consider our own lives. From the beginning of his journey, God promised Abram many offspring and great blessing. But up to when he met the Lord in his mid-seventies, Abram and his wife Sarai couldn't have children. Instead of questioning God, he immediately left everything he had always known and started moving toward the promise. That's what we do when we receive Jesus Christ as our Savior. We believe God and pull up the stakes from our old way of life. We let go of the past and take hold of faith.

I wouldn't doubt that Abram and Sarai had wanted to have children for many years. They had probably worked toward it a number of times, only to be disappointed. Had they gotten frustrated and given up before God spoke to Abram and promised to make him a great nation? I don't know. I only know Abram didn't let unfulfilled desires hold him back. Instead of ignoring God and leaning on his own ability to make things happen, he obeyed God and walked toward hope.

Abram kept moving forward, even though he had no idea how God's promise would come to pass. He kept following the Lord, though he didn't know where God was leading him. Does this sound familiar? It should, because this is the process of our walk of faith. Sometimes as we walk with God things get complicated and we lose sight of the promise.

Now let me remind you again: The end depends upon the beginning. When we encounter delays or suffer loss during our walk with the Lord, we have to trust Him just as we did when we first got saved. God didn't need our help to save us; why should He need our help to bring His promises to pass?

Have you received a promise from God that seems humanly impossible? God often tells us things that stretch our thinking beyond our comfort zones—because HE IS GOD. His thoughts and ways are much higher than ours. But Abram gave us a pattern to follow: (1) He believed God and kept moving forward on his daily journey, and (2) He kept drawing near to the Lord.

Of course, Abram's faith in God's promise was tested. It took twenty-five years before the promise came to pass. In the meantime, in Genesis 16, Sarai said to Abram: "See now, the LORD has restrained me from bearing children. Please, go in to my maid; perhaps I shall obtain children by her.' And Abram heeded the voice of Sarai" (v. 2). He moved out of faith into presumption.

When we look at our circumstances and don't see any fruit of our desired outcome, we can conclude it is God's will. We can believe He really doesn't want us to inherit that promise; therefore, we need to make it happen ourselves. Hope deferred makes the heart sick. The Hebrew root word for this expression means, " . . . to be rubbed or worn . . . (figurative) to be weak, sick, afflicted; or (causative) to grieve, make sick."[1]

Interestingly, the *Vine's Expository Dictionary* also says of this same root word: "When Samson told Delilah that if he were tied up with bowstrings he would 'be weak, and be as another man' (Judges 16:7), the verb obviously did not mean 'become sick,' unless being sick implied being less than normal for Samson."[2]

So we can glean from this that hope deferred wears down a strong heart. It weakens it to a state of grieving. From the point of view of Samson's story, hope deferred can reduce us to an overall weakened state that is less than God's best for us (that is, normal): a state in which we are unable to break loose from the enemy's chains.

Now here's our hope. A little dab will do you. God never intended for us to overcome the enemy in our own strength. He intends for us to *believe Him, come to Him,* and *obey Him.* And God does His part. He *orders our steps, reshapes our lives,* and *leads us into our destiny.* When we submit to God, we can resist the devil and he will flee from us (James 4:7). Holding on to faith is the key to letting go of private pain.

GOD'S TIMING IS PERFECT

When waiting gets tough, we need to stay in faith toward God. Otherwise, we'll end up with more grief than we bargained for. To make a long story short, Sarai's maid, Hagar, conceived and gave birth to a son whose name became Ishmael. The complications began; the baby and his mother were driven away (Genesis 16:3-14). But in spite of their mistake, when Abram was ninety-nine years old God appeared to him and said:

> I am Almighty God; walk before Me and be blameless. And I will make My covenant between Me and you, and will multiply you exceedingly. . . . No longer shall your name be called Abram, but your name shall be called Abraham; for I have made you a father of many nations. I will make you exceedingly fruitful; and I will make nations of you, and kings shall come from you. And I will establish My covenant between Me and you and your descendants after you in their generations, for an everlasting

covenant, to be God to you and your descendants after you. (Genesis 17:1-7)

This time when God repeated the promise, He added more revelation. He also added another requirement: every male child was to be circumcised as a sign of the covenant (vv. 10-14). He also told Abraham his wife's name would now be Sarah, saying: "And I will bless her, . . . and she shall be a mother of nations; kings of peoples shall be from her" (v. 16).

When God gives a promise, He knows exactly when it should come to pass. His timing is perfect. Isaac was born when Abraham was one hundred years old and he inherited the blessing. However, Abraham and Sarah had jumped the gun. Ultimately, Ishmael grew up and had children; then his children had children. Today, the descendants of Isaac and Ishmael are still fighting in the Middle East. When Abram and Sarai moved out of faith into presumption, it had far-reaching impacts.

It doesn't matter who you are, where you come from, or what you do for a living. You influence someone. Your decisions impact others. So stay in faith. Hold on to your treasure, no matter what you may have lost or may still be waiting for God to do in your life.

Let me also point out that God tells us exactly *what we need to know when the time is right.* Go back and look at how He kept expanding His promise to Abraham. Each time

Abraham was ready, after he had followed God and gained enough understanding, the Lord revealed more of His promise. And we know from reading the Bible that Isaac was born and later inherited the promise (Genesis 21:1-5; 25:11; 26:24-25). Then the promise continued to unfold in the life of Isaac's son, Jacob, whose name was later changed to Israel (Genesis 28:1-4; 32:1-30).

God keeps His promises. He kept His word then, and He still keeps His word today. So be encouraged! Real treasure endures. The light of the knowledge of the glory of God in the face of Jesus Christ is eternal.

WAIT ON THE LORD WITH EXPECTATION

You can't help God out, but you can trust Him. Take comfort knowing that God knows you better than you know yourself. If He tells you something, wait for Him to confirm His Word and lead you in the direction you should go. The question isn't whether you should wait on the Lord. The question is *how you should wait*. As we saw in Abraham's story, waiting on the Lord doesn't mean you twiddle your thumbs and do nothing. Let's read a promise from the book of Isaiah:

Have you not known? / Have you not heard? / The ever-lasting God, the LORD, / the Creator of the ends of the earth, / neither faints nor is weary. / His understanding is unsearchable. / He gives power to the weak, / and to those who have no might He increases strength. . . . / But those who wait on the LORD / shall renew their strength; / they shall mount up with wings like eagles, / they shall run and not be weary, / they shall walk and not faint. (Isaiah 40:28-29, 31)

I don't know about you, but reading this promise gives me hope! God clearly promises that when we wait on Him that He'll transform our grief. He'll turn our weakness into strength. We'll "mount up" with wings like eagles, run with endurance, and walk at a steady pace. All of the language in this passage sounds pretty active to me.

When we wait on the Lord spiritually, we continue moving forward in the natural realm. We're active and productive while we wait. Truth be told, when we truly believe the Lord is going to show up and meet a need, we prepare ourselves for it. It's just like having a houseguest. If you believe your guests are coming, as they said they were, you're going to prepare for their arrival, right?

Similarly, there should be no doubt in your mind that God is going to keep His promises. So, you stay prepared to receive them. You get up every day thanking God for loving you and giving you the breath of life. You worship Him for who He is and praise Him for what He's done. You spend time in the Word and in prayer. You love your family, attend church regularly, and actively fellowship with other believers. You work honestly and diligently to make a living and treat others the way you'd like to be treated.

When troubles arise, you stand in faith and trust God. If need be, you cry out to Him. And when you need it, you don't hesitate to get godly counsel and agreement in prayer. I'll say it again: Letting go of private pain is much easier with God than without Him.

There's nothing passive about waiting on the Lord to fulfill His Word and promises in your life. So wait with expectation, because waiting on the Lord is guarding your treasure. Having done this, you'll be sensitive to the Holy Spirit when God reveals and confirms the next step in your purpose. You'll also avoid falling prey to presumption and making rash decisions in between your present circumstances and your future promise.

As you guard your treasure, you'll rest assured that the God who worked a miracle for you in the past will do it again . . . *His way and in His timing.* That's why, when I was weak and in my darkest hour, I was able to say, "All right, Lord. You've helped me all these years; You can help me through this as well."

The grief process has many ups and downs. Sometimes a present circumstance or a painful memory can catch you by surprise and tempt you to take matters into your own hands. But God! Real treasure endures . . . you just have to wait on the Lord.

If you've lost trust and hope, don't give up. Trust again. Many times the devil will try to make you throw in the towel when your breakthrough is a breath away. As you work through your private pain, remember that God is working all things together for your good. So trust Him! He'll bring His promise to pass in your life.

FAITH CHECK

Benjamin Franklin said, "Those things that hurt, instruct."[3] Are you weary of waiting for your breakthrough? Has your pain only increased over time? Take out a pencil and your notebook or journal and get ready to put your pain in check. Real treasure endures because God transforms our weaknesses as we let go of them and hold on to faith. Keep this in mind as you work through the following questions:

1. Have you moved out of faith and into presumption? If so, what made you become impatient with God and take matters into your own hands? What were the consequences? Have you dealt with the consequences proactively, or are you still struggling in this situation?

2. Have unfulfilled desires held you back from trusting God and getting on with your life? Has hope deferred weakened your heart, making you unable to break the power of grief, or to break out of a negative cycle?

Think about how you have or haven't stayed prepared to receive God's promises. How do you need to change to begin waiting expectantly?

Now let's go to God together and submit these things to Him in prayer.

Dear Lord Jesus, we come to You again thanking You for Your love and goodness. We lay our burdens down at Your feet. Forgive us, Lord, for becoming weary while waiting for Your promise and for taking matters into our own hands. [Take a few minutes and share your responses with the Lord.] We thank You for delivering us from the pain and frustration of hope deferred and for giving us wisdom to move forward. We will obey you, Lord, because we know Your timing is perfect and You always keep your promises. In Your great name we pray. Amen.

I believe God with you today that your turnaround will be much greater than your grief, because He's working all things together for your good. Now, if you haven't done so already, take some time and reread chapter 1. You'll be ready to tackle the next chapter with a brilliant light and a song in your heart.

THE GRIEF PROCESS

Where Your Treasure Is,
Your Heart Will Be Also

And you, child, will be called the prophet of the Highest . . . to
give light to those who sit in darkness and the shadow of death,
to guide our feet into the way of peace.

LUKE 1:76, 79

Throughout the process of grieving the loss of my son, I had to go to war, both in the realm of the spirit and in my daily life. There was a battle of emotions going on inside of me. Some days I would start out strong, and then grief would come back up again. Then I'd cry out to the Lord and He'd calm me down. Dealing with private pain isn't a one-time event; it is a very human day-to-day process. As you walk through letting go of your pain, understand that it's normal to have ups and downs. It's all part of the grief cycle.

So, what does the cycle of grief look like? How long does it last? How do you know where you are in the process and when you'll come out on the other side? There are guidelines we can become aware of that are helpful; but understand, your grief experience is a personal journey. Every person is unique. Our temperaments, life experiences, strengths, weaknesses, and grief experiences are different. However, it's helpful to know what the grief cycle is in general, so we can have an idea what we're dealing with while we're going through it.

This reminds me of our friend who sang at her mother's funeral. A week or so after the funeral, when everything had calmed down, she was finally able to cry. One day while she was alone, reflecting on what had happened, her emotions erupted. She cried out in anguish for the loss of her mother; she cried for the special moments they'd had and for many others they hadn't been able to share over the years because of her mother's illness. She cried because she just didn't understand; when everything seemed to be going so well for her mother, why had she died so suddenly? Had she suffered, or did she die quickly? Why did she die alone?

She had so many unresolved feelings and unanswered questions. She couldn't stop the tears. Before long her face was soaking wet as she lay on the floor, trembling. The intense sting of pain in her heart took her completely by surprise. God had helped her so miraculously, both up to and during the funeral. Had she somehow slipped out of faith and stopped believing the Lord would bring her through? Why was this happening?

Shortly after, she started having periods of intense reflection and regret. Memories from her childhood that she had long forgotten started resurfacing in her mind . . . and some of them still hurt. And she never knew when these emotional memories were going to come up. Sometimes it happened at home or at the grocery store. Sometimes it happened at work. Many times memories resurfaced during church services while she was worshiping or listening to the pastor's message. It was happening so much she started wondering if she was unraveling. She had never experienced anything like this before.

At that time, she was working for a prominent ministry, and the Human Resources Director was a highly anointed counselor who also headed up the counseling ministry at their church. She was prompted in her spirit to ask if she could talk to him about what she was going through. They met and decided to keep meeting once a week while she was walking through her process. She said that every time she went into his office the anointing was so strong that as soon as she sat down a river of tears started to flow. I'm not certain for how long they met, but it was extremely helpful to her.

During their sessions, she learned that what she was going through was a normal part of the grief cycle. The knowledge helped her relax, trust God, and walk through the process, knowing she wasn't unraveling . . . she was releasing her private pain so she could deal with it. Ultimately, our friend came to terms with her grief. And she was able to see how God had allowed healing to come in her mother's life before He took her home.

There are no cut-and-dry answers for what you may experience during your grief cycle or exactly when you'll come out on the other side. But one thing is certain. Jesus will be with you every step of the way. He's the way, the truth, and the life (see John 14:6). If you'll trust Him and release your private pain, He'll guide you through the darkness so you'll arrive safely on the other side. He'll lead you out of turmoil to a place of peace.

UNDERSTANDING THE GRIEF CYCLE

Grief is hard. It is the root of private pain. When we're experiencing pain, it's because we are grieving a loss: a lost job, the loss of a loved one either through death or divorce, a failed business, or the loss of a home . . . the list goes on and on. We experience grief, mild to severe, when we lose anyone or anything that's important to us.

Are you heartbroken? Something is going on psychologically that is causing you to feel down and isolated: like no one understands you. Beneath all of these feelings is the root cause . . . grief. If you haven't done so until now, take a moment and trace back to the event(s) that set these feelings in motion. Private pain goes unresolved when we don't trace it back to its source. This can result in your forming negative patterns of behavior that continue for years and hinder your progress and potential. So, when you're in private pain, you need to stop and take an honest look at what's going on in your soul.

Although you love God, your pain is real . . . and as I said before, for this reason it's not going anywhere until you deal with it. Let's explore some of the things you may experience emotionally as you walk through the grief process. During this journey make it your goal and priority to not get snagged or stuck in any stage. Decide today that you're going to trust God, identify your pain, and release it—because where your treasure is, your heart will be also (Luke 12:34).

Let's start by defining grief. *Webster's American Family Dictionary* describes grief as: "keen mental suffering or distress over affliction or loss; sharp sorrow; painful regret."[1] I use an eight-step model, which has developed since Elisabeth Kübler-Ross introduced the "five stages theory" in her book, *On Death and Dying*, in 1969. The general theory is that the stages we go through during the grief process can help us learn how to live without what we have lost. The five original stages are denial, anger, bargaining, depression, and acceptance.[2] The eight stages of grief I use include:

- Shock and Denial
- Pain, Guilt, and Frustration
- Anger and Bargaining
- Depression, Reflection, and Loneliness
- The Upward Turn
- Reconstruction and Working Through
- Acceptance and Hope
- A New Beginning

The thought behind the stages of grief is that after reaching the acceptance stage, you'll begin to look forward to and plan for the future. But again, each person's experience is unique. You may or may not go through these grief stages in the same order, but they'll likely play out in one way or another. The bottom line is you need to get deliverance and healing in your stages of grief so you can move forward and get on with your life.

Let me remind you again that, as a believer, you don't have to go through this process alone. First of all, you have divine help. Second, you can get godly counsel from your pastor, a loved one, a trusted friend, or even a professional counselor. Like our friend at the beginning of this chapter, God will comfort you and show you what you need to do to work through your grief process. If He leads you to seek out counsel as she did, I encourage you to pursue it.

Now as we go into the eight stages, I want you to remember another promise from the Word of God. Psalm 34:17-19 says, "The righteous cry out, and the LORD hears, / and delivers them out of all their troubles. / The LORD is near to those who have a broken heart, / and saves such as have a contrite spirit. / Many are the afflictions of the righteous, / but the LORD delivers him out of them all."

The word *delivers* has various meanings, but as it pertains to God's deliverance, it means, "to snatch away . . . defend, deliver (self), escape . . . without fail . . . preserve, recover, rescue . . . save . . . "[3] The *Theological Wordbook of the Old Testament* adds, " . . . its basic physical sense is one of drawing out or pulling out."[4]

So as we move forward, think of it this way: When you cry out to God, He not only hears you—He *draws you* and *pulls you out* of all your troubles. He leads you and heals you as you walk through the process. Sometimes He sovereignly "snatches you out" of your afflictions, like He did on that final night the children of Israel left Egypt. But remember, God does what only He can do and you do what you can do. Most importantly, remember to cry out to God. That makes all the difference.

STAGE ONE: SHOCK AND DENIAL

When you first learn of the loss, you may react with numb disbelief or even subconsciously deny it really happened to avoid experiencing pain. This is a self-protective mechanism that keeps you from being overwhelmed. You don't want to believe what happened. You might even feel like it's all just a bad dream. Whatever you were doing at the time you experienced the loss usually gets put on hold until you can come to grips with your emotions.

When I heard of my son's death, I went numb. I remember reading the text I had received over and over again. When I called my mother, I still didn't want to believe this was actually happening to me. And I do remember thinking, *Am I dreaming? This is so surreal . . . what's going on?* By the strength of the Lord, I could still function. I was still able to go to church and finish the day's business.

However, I realize there are others who go into a state of shock after experiencing a loss, and it consumes them. They aren't able to do anything. There are times that shock is so severe, people have slipped into mental illness or have even suffered a nervous breakdown because of it. If they're already grieving, or if they have a physiological condition, they can slip into a prolonged state of shock and denial and be unable to come out of it. This is when I usually recommend they may need professional medical attention.

So, again, everyone is unique. I'm just grateful that the Lord Jesus Christ is my personal Savior. I don't know how nonbelievers handle a tragic loss without the Lord.

STAGE TWO: PAIN, GUILT, AND FRUSTRATION

Generally speaking, as the shock wears off, the sharp pain of loss starts sinking in. In some situations this pain can seem almost unbearable, so you want to escape it. Escape mechanisms to numb the pain can include physical addictions to food, drugs, alcohol, sports, or even sex. This isn't the way God wants you to deal with private pain. You need to experience the pain fully, trusting in the Lord, instead of trying to hide or soothe it. Again, the pain won't go away on its own because it's real.

You may also experience guilt, remorse, or frustration when remembering things you either did or didn't do before your loss. I had the feeling that if I had been there, my son's death would have been prevented. I wondered how I could have done more for him; how could I have been a better parent, and so on. *If only this or that didn't happen,* I thought, *he wouldn't be there in that situation.* I even remember saying, "Lord, why didn't You just take me instead of him?"

The pain hit me like a ton of bricks: a psychological anguish that I wouldn't want anyone else to experience. Whatever upsets you psychologically will eventually upset you physically as well. I began to experience chest pains, and there were times I just hurt all over. I'm sure my blood pressure also rose during that time. It was extremely painful.

In spite of everything I was going through, I stayed the course and continued to minister to others. That was a tremendous part of my healing. I'm a firm believer that as you help others, the Lord helps you. And that's exactly what the Lord did for me. As I continued to minister, and continued to live, I was able to cope. Some people turn to drugs, some people turn to alcohol, but I turned to Christ Jesus. You can as well.

I need to mention there are people who may not turn to drugs or alcohol, but they'll turn to homicide or suicide. And I had opportunity to turn to each of those areas. But I didn't. I cried out to the Lord and depended on His strength and wisdom to help me process my pain. I thank God for the power of His Word and the comfort of His presence.

STAGE THREE: ANGER AND BARGAINING

Pain, guilt, and frustration can either lead to anger, or you can experience them simultaneously. When you suffer a loss, it feels like you've been wronged; and anger, a strong feeling of displeasure and hostility, often follows. Anger releases bottled-up emotions, so it's important for you to manage your anger properly.

I mentioned before that I had feelings of wanting to get even with anyone who had any role in my son's death. I wanted to fly to California and get even. But God helped me through it. Of course, we were busy taking care of family business, making funeral arrangements, and so on. But when I thought about the fact that my two-year-old grandson had had his daddy ripped out of his life, my emotions flared up.

I was in pain and angry with God. I said, "Wow, Lord. I'll just stop preaching. If You're going to take mine, let me just stop doing what I'm doing . . . I'll quit and just go back into the world." Satan really tries to play mind games with you during the grief process. I was so angry with God I was tempted to quit—just give up on everybody and everything and leave so nobody would know where I was. So many feelings came up inside of me; but thankfully, I didn't entertain them for long.

I can laugh about it now. Actually, the Lord and I had a good laugh about it together. I said, "Lord, You created me. You know this flesh." And I believe He said to me, "Now, you know that sounded ridiculous." Of course, it did. Why would anyone in their right mind try to strike such a confrontational bargain with the Lord? And although I had opportunity to mismanage my anger, I'm so glad He shined His light in my soul. By God's grace, instead of doing something drastic, I chose to do Jesus.

When you're in pain and angry about your loss, try not to lash out and blame someone else. The Lord is strong enough to handle your grief, but another person may not be. If you give full vent to your anger, you could potentially cause permanent damage in a relationship. Grief strains relationships enough as it is. Marriages have ended after parents suffered the loss of a child because they couldn't get beyond anger and blame.

In fact, I believe all relationships are challenged when we're grieving. All of my relationships were challenged in one way or another. That's why I urge you, no matter what circumstances and emotions you're dealing with, *cry out to God for help*. He can comfort you like no other. He can give you mind-boggling peace as He *draws you* and *pulls you out* of your affliction. I'm thankful that God hears the cries of our hearts and doesn't condemn us. He understands our pain much better than we realize.

STAGE FOUR: DEPRESSION, REFLECTION, AND LONELINESS

When you get through the initial stages of your loss and some time has passed, you could experience a long period of sad reflection. This is normal. People who love you and care about your well-being may try to console you and make you feel better. But at this point, you may not be responsive to it. By the time you reach this stage, you've thought about a lot of things and realize the full magnitude of your loss. Then you can become depressed.

When you are depressed, you're disheartened about your situation. You're sad and gloomy and at times even withdrawn from others. You may isolate yourself on purpose, reflecting on your memories. Then you end up feeling lonely and empty because you know it's over. All has been said and done, and there's no way you can bring it back.

I knew people meant well when they consoled me. Sometimes it was just difficult for me to hear it. When you're in this stage, you don't want to be encouraged. You don't want to hear church jargon. Sometimes you don't want anyone to come up to you and say anything at all, not even, "I'm praying for you" or "Hey, how are you doing?" I know this may sound harsh, but when you're walking through this stage, struggling to not lose hope, hearing these things doesn't seem to help . . . nevertheless, it's the right thing to hear.

Granted, many people who say they'll pray for you may not. And some people are just being polite when they ask how you're doing. So trust God and keep your chin up. When it feels like you're losing all hope, trust again. You still have the breath of life, the light of Jesus, within you. Sometimes, knowing this is all that matters.

I remember there were times I felt people were watching me for my reaction. Would I break down in tears and grieve in front of them? I didn't want to put my grief on display, even though some people encouraged me to stop being strong and let it out. Many times I didn't want to hear that because I'm strong and I was depending on the Lord. But I realize it helps some people feel better about your pain if they actually see you grieve. For me to share details of my private pain with members of our congregation, though I love them deeply, would have to be under the unction of the Lord. And as you know, that time came two years after my son died.

But again, everyone handles pain differently. I'm not knocking those who grieve in public, and I'm not judging those who don't express their private pain. I'm sure the royal family in Great Britain suffered deep pain at the loss of Diana, but we didn't see it publicly. One thing is true: It doesn't matter if you're aristocratic or if you're dirt poor, pain isn't prejudiced. Pain doesn't discriminate. We do need to identify and release our pain, however, in order to keep moving forward.

Oftentimes, there are some people who just don't know what to say, and that's okay. When you're grieving, especially when you're in this stage of depression, reflection, and loneliness, there are times when just having someone there is all you need. Words aren't necessary—just a caring face and, when the time is right, perhaps a shoulder to cry on.

STAGE FIVE: THE UPWARD TURN

Ultimately your life starts coming back into balance and your emotions begin to clarify. The shock is gone. Pain, guilt, and frustration are no longer getting the best of you. You've worked through your anger, and you're no longer trying to strike a bargain with God. Depression, reflection, and loneliness have lifted enough so that you can get a glimpse of the future beyond your pain. Spiritually speaking, this is when God starts stirring your treasure chest . . . you can sense things are taking a turn for the better.

This actually happened to me several times. The first time it happened, the pain of my son's loss was still fresh; but the Lord allowed me to preview my upward turn at his funeral. When the preacher extended an altar call, I was led to get up. As I extended the invitation for others to accept Jesus Christ into their hearts, I felt prompted to share some of my pain through the Word of God.

I told everyone how important it is to have a relationship with God through Jesus Christ, and not just "child support." You see, when children receive support from their natural fathers, it doesn't necessarily mean they have a relationship. I stressed the importance of having a covenant relationship with God, our heavenly Father, instead of being satisfied to just receive child support (i.e., His blessings).

Half of the people in the service that day came to the altar to make a decision for Jesus Christ. It felt wonderful to see

God move so powerfully in people's hearts. Before I sat back down, I reminded the audience of Larry's last assignment— to get everyone into the house of the Lord so those standing at the altar could make a decision for Christ. Yielding to the unction of the Lord that day helped me tremendously. It was the beginning of my upward turn.

You may or may not have a similar experience, but you'll know when it happens. If you're like me, it may happen several times. So be encouraged! Things can, and will, get better as you trust in the Lord. His timing is perfect.

STAGE SIX: RECONSTRUCTION AND WORKING THROUGH

Now you're becoming more functional, especially so if you've allowed the Lord to guide you through the process. You discover, though your vision may have been suppressed for a season, it has never left you. With God's grace and direction, you start looking for realistic solutions and rebuilding your life. This stage actually began for me after the funeral. When I saw those souls coming to the altar, I got a revelation for my situation. My assignment for this season became clearer. The devil had stolen from me, and I was going on the offense. I was going to go deep into his territory and win back every soul God allowed.

I immediately began to restructure my personal ministry, as well as our church, Praise Temple Full Gospel Baptist Cathedral, where I serve as senior pastor. I started lining everything up so I could announce to our congregation: "We're going after souls for the kingdom by any means necessary." I didn't want anyone to suffer the pain I was coming through without the strength and help of the Lord.

Everything changed for me at my son's funeral, even my relationship with Christ. To my amazement, it was strengthened. It got better, in spite of my pain and weaknesses. Before my son passed away, I thought that I had a strong relationship with the Lord. Then this tragedy exposed the areas where I was weak and needed to improve. And so, the restructuring came. I have a new and improved life in Christ Jesus.

I encourage you, when you reach this stage to really take a deep look at your life. Evaluate and reevaluate every person, place, and thing around you. Let God restore your vision, and then start restructuring your life. You can do it!

STAGE SEVEN:
ACCEPTANCE AND HOPE

You've finally reached the stage where you've come to terms with your grief and learned to accept your loss. From this vantage point, you can have renewed hope for the future.

Bear in mind, you may not be instantly happy, but you'll be content and at peace. Don't expect or even try to return to where you were before your loss. With God's help, you'll keep moving toward your destiny, strengthened with renewed perspective and purpose.

I'm sure you're probably familiar with the well-known "Serenity Prayer," which states: *"God, grant me the serenity to accept the things I cannot change; courage to change the things I can; and wisdom to know the difference."*[5] I have learned to accept what God has allowed. I have accepted the fact that there's nothing I can do to bring my son back. I can only hit the reset button, restart from where I am, and go forward.

A dear friend of mine, we call him Bishop Richard "Mr. Clean" White, sang a song with Evangelist Twinkie Clark entitled, "Accept What God Allows."[6] I'm able to do this because He's much greater than I am. He knows much more than I know, and all power is in His hands. He's the treasure in my soul that gives me light, life, hope, joy, and eternal purpose. Because of this, I can keep moving forward. Because of this, I know you can do the same.

STAGE EIGHT: A NEW BEGINNING

What do I need to say about a new beginning? The words speak for themselves. Everything is new again. Having dealt with private pain and come through to the other side of your grief, you can truly have a fresh start: an even more promising beginning—because as you trusted God in the midst of your pain, you gained strength, wisdom, and insight from your experience.

I've heard it said many times and have said myself that you can't move forward until you get out of the past. So believe God and press on! Don't get stuck in any stage of the grief cycle. I believe I'm a better man and a more seasoned, effective minister because God allowed this situation to take place in my life. I'm moving beyond my private pain, reminding myself daily that none of us will live forever.

FAITH CHECK

American writer and publisher Elbert Hubbard said, "The cure for grief is motion."[7] To this I say, *yes indeed.* Moving forward through each stage of the grief process is essential. And as you hold on to your faith, it is entirely possible because the Lord faithfully *draws you* and *pulls you out* of all your troubles.

Holding on to faith in God while letting go of private pain is an ongoing process in every believer's life—this is why the light of Jesus can shine so brilliantly from within us.

As I close this chapter, I want you to think about your loss and which stage(s) of the grief cycle you've come through up to this point. Now check your faith: Have you cried out to

God each time you felt the sting of pain? Have you released your pain to Him in each stage of the process? Finally, have you kept moving forward, obediently doing what He prompts you to do by His Holy Spirit?

If so, I commend you for waiting in expectancy in the face of adversity. If not, I don't condemn you, and neither does the Lord. Now, regardless of how you answered the questions, take some time to write your feelings about where you are right now in your journal. Use them as a springboard to cry out to the Lord in prayer because He's the treasure that keeps your heart intact. When you come out of your prayer closet, hold on to faith by doing what He leads you to do. Let me pray for you:

Faithful Father, I bless Your name, for You are great and greatly to be praised. Thank You for being near to my friend who has suffered a painful loss and is coming through the grief process. Hear the cries of his or her heart. Give comfort, peace, wisdom, and strength, Lord. Renew hope, vision, and purpose. I thank You for delivering my friend out of many troubles and for doing what only You can do. I thank You that a brand-new beginning is on the way, and that You're giving my friend the strength and resolve to keep moving forward. Thank You for guiding our feet into the way of peace. In the matchless name of Jesus I pray. Amen.

CHAPTER 6

OVERTURNING CIRCUMSTANTIAL EVIDENCE

Discovering the Hidden Treasures of God

My son, if you receive my words,
and treasure my commands within you,
so that you incline your ear to wisdom,
and apply your heart to understanding; . . .
if you seek her as silver,
and search for her as for hidden treasures;
then you will understand the fear of the LORD,
and find the knowledge of God. . . .
He is a shield to those who walk uprightly.

PROVERBS 2:1-2, 4-5, 7b

Now that we've focused in on the grief process, I'd like to broaden our perspective. There are times when the "facts" of our circumstances seem so evident that they confront our faith in God. This is particularly true when working through the stages of grief. I remember while I was praying one day I heard myself say, "Lord, I don't mind waiting, but it's the happenings while I wait that are driving me crazy."

As we go through each stage of releasing private pain, we must understand: It's not what we look at that matters but what we can see through the eyes of faith. God has immeasurable wisdom. His knowledge and commands are a safe place of refuge for us. So it's vital for us to seek Him: to receive His words, treasure His commands, listen to His wisdom, and apply it to our hearts. No matter what we may lose in this life, nothing can take away this infinite hidden treasure in our souls.

Strong faith in God—not faith in faith or faith in people—overturns circumstantial evidence. It helps us to see what is true when all evidence appears to be to the contrary.

In the legal field, circumstantial evidence is a common term. The word *circumstantial* is anything "pertaining to or derived from circumstances."[1] *Circumstantial evidence* is "proof of facts offered as evidence from which other facts are to be inferred [speculated]"[2] [emphasis mine].

In other words, circumstantial evidence looks real because it's based on the facts of your circumstances—what seems obvious to you when you look at it—but there's no other proof to support it. It's up to you to arrive at a conclusion, whether or not your circumstances are true, by speculating in your mind. That's exactly what the enemy wants.

God doesn't want us to arrive at conclusions this way. That's why He sent Jesus—the way, the truth, and the life— to shine His eternal light in our inner man. Instead of looking at our circumstances and determining that's just the way things are going to be, He wants us to seek Him in our circumstances and discover the truth. So, instead of being overcome by our circumstances, we overturn circumstantial evidence and God transforms the outcome.

Jesus said: "Ask, and it will be given to you; seek, and you will find; knock, and it will be opened to you. For everyone who asks receives, and he who seeks finds, and to him who knocks it will be opened" (Matthew 7:7-8). We are partners with Him in our daily experience. He is the treasure within us, and we are stewards of our souls. I'll say it again: We do what we can do, and God does what only He can do.

While we're waiting on the Lord and working through our private pain, we're confronted with all kinds of evidence. That's where our faith comes in. The devil tries to make us think our circumstances are impossible to deny. But when we're waiting with expectancy (as I shared in chapter 4), staying prepared to receive the promises of God, we're able to see and move beyond our private pain.

The enemy's circumstantial evidence can be pretty compelling. For example, after God delivered the Israelites out of

Egypt (symbolizing the world), they were confronted by Pharaoh and his army as they approached the Red Sea (Exodus 14:10-12). The people had overwhelming circumstantial evidence they weren't going to make it to the other side. All evidence to the contrary, God intervened and delivered His people out of their troubles (vv. 13-31).

When you're recovering from a tremendous loss, there are times when it looks like a massive Red Sea is in front of you. You feel like you may never get to the other side of your grief. That's circumstantial evidence. While it's a fact that you'll be confronted by many strong emotions during your grief cycle, you can see beyond your pain through faith in God. You can trust God and partner with Him. Ask, seek, and knock.

Think about it this way. When the Israelites were sandwiched between the Red Sea and Pharaoh's army, the Lord said to Moses:

> Why do you cry to Me? Tell the children of Israel to go forward. But lift up your rod, and stretch out your hand over the sea and divide it. And the children of Israel shall go on dry ground through the midst of the sea. And I indeed will harden the hearts of the Egyptians, and they shall follow them. So I will gain honor over Pharaoh and over all his army, his chariots, and his horsemen. Then the Egyptians shall know that I am the LORD, when I have gained honor for Myself over Pharaoh, his chariots, and his horsemen. (Exodus 14:15-18)

Moses' part was to obey God, tell the people to go forward, lift up his rod, and stretch out his hand over the sea. God's part was to give Moses the strategy and, when Moses did what He'd told him to do, to create a path for the Israelites to walk on dry ground all the way to the other side. Then when the people obeyed and moved forward, God hardened the enemy's heart so he'd order his army to pursue them. Later, Moses stretched out his hand over the sea again at God's command, and He drowned Pharaoh's army in the midst of the sea (vv. 21-29).

What a dynamic, productive partnership. God did what only He could do, and Moses obeyed and did his part. Then the children of Israel obeyed and moved forward, and God won a victory over Israel's enemy. They trusted the Lord, overturned circumstantial evidence, and God transformed their outcome. This same principle works for you and me. Why? Jesus Christ is the same yesterday, today, and forever.

You can do all things through Christ who strengthens you! I encourage you to actively partner with God as you work through private pain. This starts with knowing Him intimately, just as Moses did. When we seek the rich treasures of God in God's presence, He gladly gives us His wisdom. He gives us strategies to overturn our circumstances and makes a clear path for us to walk on, so we'll keep moving forward into victory.

Finally, when the Israelites saw the great work God had done, three things happened: (1) They *feared* the Lord;

(2) they *believed* the Lord and His servant Moses; and (3) they *sang a song* of deliverance and victory. (See Exodus 14:30–15:21.) Keeping a song in our hearts seals the victory. As we move forward, let me remind you of our victory song: "This Little Light of Mine."

Everywhere you go, especially now as you're working through private pain, you have the blessed opportunity to let your light, your treasure, shine brightly in darkness. I declare to you according Daniel 11:32 that "the people who know their God shall be strong, and carry out great exploits." Are you with me? The Lord is willing and well able to transform overwhelming circumstances into life-changing experiences as we believe Him.

MANAGING YOUR SOUL

Remember, the Lord is the treasure within you, and you are the steward of your soul. How can you partner with God in your deliverance? Manage your soul. That's your part of the deliverance process. I've touched on this in earlier chapters, especially in chapter 3 when we dealt with public masks and images in our minds. I also gave a few pointers toward the end of chapter 4 when I talked about the things we do when we wait on the Lord with expectancy.

Now we're going to focus in on our part of walking with the Lord daily, which contributes greatly to our success in coming through the grief process. First of all, we need to understand we are in a spiritual battle. The devil is the enemy of our souls. This has already been well established up to this point. But we also have to wage war against our flesh (our own unique "in-a-me") and resist worldly influences.

My booklet, *30 Minutes in Prayer*, focuses on developing a lifestyle of prayer, praise, holy meditation, and true worship. Allow me to speak to you from its pages: "Keep in mind, regardless of how long you've known God, your 'flesh' (sinful nature) will try to pull you back into your lifestyle before you knew Him. Your spirit hungers and thirsts for God, but your flesh only wants to satisfy its earthly desires. If you follow the dictates of your flesh it won't be long before you stop seeking God."[3]

Galatians 5:17 says: "The flesh lusts against the Spirit, and the Spirit against the flesh; and these are contrary to one another, so that you do not do the things that you wish." When you follow the dictates of your flesh, you're playing right into the enemy's hands. If you don't manage your soul, you won't do your part in partnering with the Lord. Not only will this compromise your intimacy with God, it will also affect your ability to overturn circumstantial evidence and come all the way through the grief cycle.

You are responsible for the management of your soul, so I encourage you to trust God and manage well. It's amazing how we often don't pay attention to something until we lose it. This happens physically, as well as spiritually and soulishly (psychologically). Our flesh demands attention, so we put other areas on the back burner. We sit in barber shops and beauty shops getting our hair and nails groomed, we go to the gym and do aerobics, lift weights, and so on, taking care of our physical well-being. Sometimes we take care of our bodies, but our spirits and our souls may be neglected.

Now, don't get me wrong. It's important to take care of ourselves. But we need to guard against getting out of balance. First Thessalonians 5:23 says: "Now may the God of peace Himself sanctify you completely; and may your whole spirit, soul, and body be preserved blameless at the coming of our Lord Jesus Christ." God is concerned with every area of our lives, but notice the order of priority in the Bible verse: spirit, soul, and then the body.

Maintaining our relationship with God is the foundation of managing our souls and bodies. Jesus said, "Watch and pray, lest you enter into temptation. The spirit indeed is willing, but the flesh is weak" (Matthew 26:41). On the practical side, this means you need to manage your priorities so you make time to feed and develop your spirit. This includes making time to pray and read the Word daily, as well as regularly attending church.

I strongly recommend that you start each day with the Lord. Finding a quiet place where you'll be undisturbed is very helpful. Once there, close your eyes and think of how magnificent He is and what He's done in your life—that will lead you into worship. Let it flow. Then let the Holy Spirit guide you into prayer. Just relax and talk to God. If you need to, use Jesus' model prayer in Matthew 6:9-13. Make sure to allow some time to listen as well. God loves revealing His hidden treasures in the secret place of prayer.

Again, a little dab will do you. I always tell people if you can start by praying just thirty minutes a day, you can build from there. This will set the atmosphere within you to be sensitive to the Holy Spirit and filter the evidence that is presented to your mind. This prepares you to more readily discern between circumstantial facts and eternal truths.

Reading the Word daily is equally important. Psalm 119:162 says, "I rejoice at Your word as one who finds great treasure." In his booklet, *Let the Journey Begin*, senior pastor, author and radio host, Jeff Wickwire writes: "Nothing is more important in your new Christian life than reading God's Word. You wouldn't consider going a day without eating. You should view Bible reading the same way. . . . God's Word is spiritual food and sustenance for your soul."[4] Whether you've walked with the Lord for years or have just gotten saved, reading the Bible is as foundational as milk for a baby and meat for sustained development and growth.

Finally, attending church regularly is essential. It's important to be under apostolic leadership, even if you pastor a church yourself. If you don't have spiritual oversight that is appointed by God to watch for your soul, I encourage you to make it a matter of prayer. When this is in place, make sure you're submitted to that leadership and authority. (See Hebrews 13:17.) This will provide spiritual connection and covering for you that is key to your growth as a believer and your effectiveness in God's kingdom. Always remember, however, God expects you to be the manager of your soul.

As you may know, many churches meet on Sundays, as well as one evening during the week. You'll learn more about God and His Word and be able to worship and fellowship with other believers. No one is an island. We need God and each other, especially when times are tough. So, even if you have a demanding schedule at home, school, or work, you need to place a high priority on being actively involved in church. This equips you for your personal ministry, trains you about life in God's kingdom, and prepares you for the future when everyone who knows the Lord will be together for eternity.

If you have physical limitations or are elderly and have difficulty getting to church, some ministries provide transportation. Many churches now offer online streaming of their services and ways to connect with them through their website. A number of churches also have regular small group meetings that are held in the homes of their members; this is a good way to develop relationships on a smaller scale and stay vitally connected to the church's overall vision. And, of course, a growing number of churches either televise or broadcast their services on the radio.

There are many options available to you. Just make sure you're personally connected by relationship. Don't be satisfied with staying on the fringe and being an observer. Get in there and get actively involved in Body life!

Developing these three spiritual disciplines nourishes your soul and equips you to overturn circumstantial evidence. Now here's another powerful promise. Galatians 6:7-8 says: "Do not be deceived, God is not mocked; for whatever a man sows, that he will also reap. For he who sows to his flesh will of the flesh reap corruption, but he who sows to the Spirit will of the Spirit reap everlasting life."

I want to reap of the Spirit, don't you? You might say this is easier said than done. To this I would say it's easier when *said and done*. Just be willing to take the first step and the Lord will help you. When you sow, you reap.

Now let's see what the Bible says about your soul. Third John 2 says, "Beloved, I pray that you may prosper in all things and be in health, just as your soul prospers." Remember, your being is comprised of spirit, soul, and body. Your soul is the gateway to both your spirit and your body, so it's important to be a good steward (manager) of your soul—especially when you're working through the challenges of life. When you feed your spirit and nourish your soul, everything prospers.

You should also make it a priority to feed your mind with positive things. Philippians 4:8-9 tells us:

Finally, brethren, whatever things are true, whatever things are noble, whatever things are just, whatever things are pure, whatever things are lovely, whatever things are of good report, if there is any virtue and if there is anything praiseworthy—meditate [think] on these things . . . and the God of peace will be with you.

We have to be deliberate about what we allow to enter our minds, especially when we're working through the stages of grief. As I counsel in my prayer booklet,

[W]e need to be watchful about what see, hear, feel and think. If we allow the wrong things to enter our minds through our natural senses, it could get us off track with God. We must be deliberate and allow only those things that are of God to cycle through our minds. There is great power in holy meditation, and there is real danger in meditating on earthly, sensual things—so be careful about what you watch on television, listen to on the radio, or give audience to when you are with your family, friends and peers.[5]

I had to step up my spiritual disciplines after my son passed away. I had to feed my spirit and fill my mind with any and everything that was positive. I had to surround myself with positive people. I had to be intentional, deliberate, because if I slacked spiritually, I could have lost my mind. There are people who have become mentally disturbed after suffering a relatively minor loss in their lives. I thank God that after suffering the loss of my son, I still have a sound mind.

We need to maintain balance by managing our souls, which means setting priorities to take care of our spirits, souls, and bodies equally. We need a holistic approach. We shouldn't do more for one than we do for the other, but we should manage our disciplines in the right order. There's no need to be spiritually strong and physically weak. In kind, there's no need to be physically strong and spiritually or psychologically weak. It's important to take care of ourselves and do the necessary things to ensure we stay close to God and keep moving forward.

Finally, to manage our souls we should seek help, counsel, and support when needed. I've mentioned this throughout the book, but I want to make sure to give you practical options. First of all, if there's a counseling ministry in your church, whether it's administered by your pastor or someone on the church staff, take advantage of it. There are also excellent Christian counseling ministries you could look into, like Focus on the Family and Meier Clinics, for example. Over and above this, there are also very reputable counseling services and agencies in the community.

If you don't know offhand where to begin, ask someone you know to recommend a service to you, or do a search on the Internet. I'm confident you'll be able to find the help you need.

Because again, when you're dealing with private pain you need to find someone to release it to. When you internalize things you can become irritable and bitter, and may end up taking your frustrations out on others, especially those who love you and are closest to you. For this reason, there are times I encourage loved ones to go to counseling as well, so someone who is objective can give them clarity about the challenges you're dealing with. This way, they'll know how to stand with you and pray for you, instead of shooting in the dark.

Sometimes the people who love you the most can think they're helping you, but they're actually hurting you because they're either unaware of what to do or are ill-advised. So I appreciate and encourage group counsel when needed; that way you'll have a team effort that will help support you while giving your loved ones the needed perspective to weather the process.

Seeking help, counsel, and support also helps you realize you're not the weird one, the weak one, or the only one dealing with private pain. Others are also facing challenges. Although their experience may not be exactly like yours, I'm certain you'll find others who are facing similar situations. Getting counsel confirms to you that you're not alone or isolated, which can be a great source of comfort.

It's incumbent upon you to seek help, to reach outside of yourself, when you're working through private pain. If you feel like no one is reaching out to you, then reach out to them. There's somebody that can help you, guide you, comfort you, and support you. But again, you have to take a risk, open your heart, remove your public mask and let someone in.

I have to give credit to the Roman Catholic Church because they have confession booths. Call it wrong or right if you want to, but they still offer a vehicle for people to reach out and talk about their problems. It's important for us to talk out our feelings and really pour out our hearts at times—because I don't think we get enough of that in the church.

As I said before, listening is an area that needs to be developed in the body of Christ. Too often, when someone needs to release private pain, a well-intentioned hearer listens for a few seconds and then wants to interject. But there are times when we just need to talk things out, and the hearer doesn't need to say a word. Listening is the heart of counseling. We need more listeners in the family of God.

If by chance you're not saved and are reading this book, I encourage you to find someone that you feel comfortable talking to. Seek assistance from a trusted family member, a friend, or even an agency. Perhaps there's a local agency you can reach out to, just to talk. (Of course, if you don't know Jesus, I highly recommend you get to know Him. I suggest you go back and read chapter 1, and make sure to complete the Faith Check.)

The bottom line is, if you're suffering from private pain, you're not in this by yourself. There's somebody out there who genuinely cares and can help you. Check out your options, and then follow through.

Self-help is another way to seek expert counsel and support. When you're challenged in an area, go buy a book and read up on it. Find a biblical teaching series that addresses the area of your struggle. As you expand your knowledge, you can likely identify and seek a broader range of solutions. Of course, make sure to guard your treasure. Avoid venturing outside of your biblical beliefs and exploring New Age or other forms of earthly meditation, such as those associated with eastern religions that are rooted in worshiping self or other gods.

As you feed your soul and meditate on (think about) things that are true, noble, just, pure, lovely, of good report, and praiseworthy, according to Philippians 4:8-9, begin to release the treasure within—speak your faith! The God of peace will be with you. He'll partner with you to bring healing and deliverance.

Proper management is key. We need to be deliberate and intentional in managing our souls. We need to make sure that our spirits are close to God, our souls are healthy, and our bodies are strong to carry out everything we need to do—especially when all evidence appears to the contrary. Then when challenges come, we won't have to struggle as long or work as hard to make it through the grief process.

It's just like housecleaning. When you keep up with it daily, things stay nice and tidy. But if you wait for a month before cleaning, it will take a lot more time and effort. So, feed your spirit every day, here a little and there a little, and when challenges come you'll be able to stand. I'll say it again: A little dab will do you.

CONFESSING THE TRUTH

Another way to overturn circumstantial evidence is by declaring truth: that is, confessing your faith through the Word of God. When you've sown to the Spirit and managed your soul wisely, this happens very naturally. But when you've sown to your fleshly nature, it feels awkward and presumptuous to speak the Word of God over your situation. Your ease or difficulty in this area is a good indicator of whether you're guarding your treasure or hiding it.

I firmly believe in confessing the Word. When you speak the promises of God, it not only strengthens you, it also goes out into the spiritual atmosphere. If you recall, when I got over the initial shock of hearing about my son's passing, I was overwhelmed with pain, became angry, and vented my frustration to the Lord. Then God mercifully spoke to my spirit and comforted me. He always speaks the truth of His Word, and His words always get results. Isaiah 55:10-11 declares:

> For as the rain comes down, and the snow from heaven, / and do not return there, / but water the earth, / and make it bring forth and bud, / that it may give seed to the sower / and bread to the eater, / so shall My word be that goes forth from My mouth; / it shall not return to Me void, / but it shall accomplish what I please, / and it shall prosper in the thing for which I sent it.

Knowing this, we should endeavor to come into agreement with God by declaring His Word over our situations. We can do this in prayer, as well as conversationally during the course of our day. For example, if someone were to say to you, "You should find whoever caused you to suffer this loss and make them pay for it," you could respond: "I'm hurting, but I'm going to trust God to help me forgive them because I know I may need forgiveness someday. If I forgive them, God will forgive me when I need it." (See Matthew 6:14-15.)

You don't always have to remember the exact chapter and verse, but when you manage your spirit wisely, the Holy Spirit will bring the Word of God back to your remembrance. When that happens, sow to the Spirit and declare the truth by speaking your faith through the Word of God.

Now I would be remiss if I didn't mention this. I'm not trying to point at any denomination or group, but there was a season in the body of Christ when we widely confessed "name it, claim it." Well, God forbid if someone got into a car accident and his or her arm got chopped off. Would looking at the ground and declaring, "I don't receive that, my arm is still attached to my shoulder" make a difference? No! We have to keep it real and avoid falling into presumption. Instead, someone should call 9-1-1 and then confess the Word: "Lord, Your Word says by Your stripes we are healed; we believe You for divine healing."

I believe in confessing the Word, but before I confess it, I admit that I have an issue. If you've suffered a tragic loss and are struggling with depression, keep it real and confess: "Lord, I'm challenged with depression and I'm speaking Your Word . . . You are my peace." But if you practiced "name it, claim it," you'd say, "I don't receive this," and then expect the problem to go away. You could try to convince yourself that you're not depressed, but that's not faith. That's called suppression, which can be much like denial. Real problems don't go away until you deal with them.

The Word of God is active and effective. It is tested, proven, and productive. The Word of God is treasure in your soul and a shield that protects your spirit, soul, and body. It is one of the formidable weapons in your spiritual arsenal: the "sword of the Spirit" (read about your spiritual armor in Ephesians 6:13-18). Notice the sword is empowered by the Spirit of God, not by human skills, strength, or abilities. So we need to make sure we come into agreement with God to use this weapon wisely. And because of what Jesus has done for us on the cross, it is fatal to the enemy.

WHAT CAN YOU SEE?

If the happenings while you wait on the Lord are driving you crazy, I encourage you to see your situation through the eyes of faith. Although the facts of your circumstances may often confront your faith in God, you can wait expectantly, manage your soul, and partner with Him to overturn circumstantial evidence.

As I prepare to close this chapter, I'd like to focus on one more aspect of seeing. In Jeremiah 1:11-12, the young prophet wrote, "Moreover the word of the LORD came to me, saying, 'Jeremiah, what do you see?' And I said, 'I see a branch of an almond tree.' Then the LORD said to me, 'You have seen well, for I am ready to perform My word.' " Almond trees bloom in Israel as early as January and February. They are an early reminder that winter is about to end and spring is on the way.

As it concerns coming through the grief cycle, are you more focused on what you've been through or where you're going? Are you seeing out of an optimistic or a pessimistic eye? I challenge you: Dare to see the truth of your situation through the optimistic eye of faith in God. New life is just ahead of you—because God watches over His Word and keeps His promises.

FAITH CHECK

John Adams, the second American president, said: "Grief drives men into habits of serious reflection, sharpens the understanding, and softens the heart."[6] I believe this is not only a fact, it is truth, don't you agree? Now, get your journal handy and take some quiet time to reflect on and answer the following questions.

1. Consider the order of priority in managing your soul: spirit, soul, and body. How well are you doing at maintaining your priorities and managing your soul? Which areas either need to be set in place or brought back into balance? Meditate on (think about) this, collect your thoughts, and then write them in your journal.

2. Consider your private pain. Do you think seeking counsel would be beneficial for you? Why or why not? Record your thoughts.

3. How would you rate yourself as it concerns confessing truth; that is, confessing your faith by praying and declaring the Word of God? Does it come to you naturally, or do you feel awkward and presumptuous when attempting to say what the Bible says? Check your faith, and then write what you discover in your journal. If need be, make managing your soul a top priority until God's hidden treasures begin to flow out of your inner person.

Of course, you also need to make each of these areas a matter of prayer. Let's start by agreeing in prayer:

Father God, we're so grateful and privileged to come into Your presence. We thank You that, according to Your wisdom and will, Jesus is the treasure within us and we are the stewards of our souls. We thank You that we can come to You in faith and ask, seek, and knock, knowing You'll hear and respond to us. Stir our souls to receive Your words and treasure Your commands, Lord. Guide us in inclining our ears to Your wisdom and applying our hearts to understanding. Show us Your hidden treasures. Help us sow to the Spirit, partner with You, and overturn circumstantial evidence. We thank You for giving us a clear path to victory because Your Word always accomplishes Your purpose. In the mighty name of Jesus we pray. Amen.

Here's a final thing for you to think about. I deliberately sandwiched the chapter about the grief cycle (chapter 5) between waiting on the Lord (chapter 4) and partnering with Him (this chapter). Because *waiting on* and *partnering with* the Lord work together to bring you all the way through to the other side of grief. All evidence to the contrary.

CHAPTER 7

IS THIS FAITH OR AM I CRAZY?

The Treasure of Trusting God

We are hard-pressed on every side, yet not crushed;
we are perplexed, but not in despair; persecuted,
but not forsaken; struck down, but not
destroyed—always carrying about in the body the
dying of the Lord Jesus, that the life of Jesus
also may be manifested in our body.

2 CORINTHIANS 4:8-10

The longer we walk with God, the more we deal with paradoxes: apparent contradictions to our faith. At times this circumstantial evidence takes us by surprise but not so with the Lord. He established this principle in the beginning. Consider this again with me. At the beginning of creation, for all appearance' sake, there was only dense darkness, an indiscernible mass of empty waste, and deep waters. But the Spirit of the Lord was hovering there, waiting with expectation, to separate light from darkness according to His master plan.

Only the Lord could imagine that light and life could come out of this. Certainly, only He could execute it.

This same spiritual dynamic works in our lives, especially when we experience private pain. God is always there . . . watching over us, looking into our troubles, and knowing the end from the beginning: patiently waiting to release light and life. God isn't worried when we're challenged on every side. His plan won't fail, and He never leaves us without help.

Why do we sometimes doubt that God can speak life into our situations? There are times, even when we faithfully manage our souls, that we're caught unaware and allow facts to overrule our faith. There are moments when we look at our problems instead of seeing God's promises and speak our frustrations instead of declaring God's truth. Yet in all of these things, God isn't challenged. He's perfecting our faith and working all things together for our good.

Let me encourage you today that being *hard-pressed, perplexed,* and *struck down* can't cancel God's will and purpose for your life. Your private pain and grief can't keep His promises from coming to pass. You will heal and be able to get on with your life.

Even when you feel like darkness is all around you, it doesn't mean the enemy has frustrated God's plan because frustration implies defeat. God isn't capable of being defeated. Light always overcomes darkness, even when all evidence is to the contrary.

Now hear me carefully: God knows the end from the beginning, so even when we suffer loss or temporary setbacks, He remains the same—because He is the truth. Our challenges don't cause Him to worry or waiver. While we're going through the processes of life, God sees our victory on the other side. He knows exactly when, according to His plan, He'll turn the tables on the enemy. So we must partner with Him and do our part: believe Him, come to Him, and obey Him.

The devil, the enemy of our souls, can't refute that God still hovers over dark situations. And he trembles at the prospect that at any moment, God will declare light into darkness and overturn his wicked schemes.

I praise God that He's the ultimate authority of speaking light and releasing life, or we wouldn't have assurance that we'll be with Him for eternity. And we couldn't have hope in the face of our challenges, knowing that better days are ahead. Paradox is a reality in our walk of faith because without a paradox, there's no need for faith in God.

GOD IS BUILDING A LEGACY

When we experience pain, trusting God, He uses it to perfect our faith and accomplish His purpose. So I encourage you again: Let go of your pain and hold on to faith because the end depends upon the beginning.

Having faith in the face of adversity seems crazy to the world and to the natural mind. But God! He takes the foolish things of the world and confounds the wise. First Corinthians 1:27-29 says:

> God has chosen the foolish things of the world to put to shame the wise, and God has chosen the weak things of the world to put to shame the things that are mighty; and the base things of the world and the things which are despised God has chosen, and the things which are not, to bring to nothing the things that are, that no flesh should glory in His presence.

You may recall in chapter 4 when I talked about Abram (who later received a new name, Abraham). It may have seemed crazy when God told him to leave his family and everything he had known to go to an unknown place. Nevertheless, God called him out of his comfort zone and away from his former covering and protection. What's really amazing is that Abram's family didn't even worship God; when his father Terah was alive, they worshiped other gods (see Joshua 24:2-3).

But as only He can do, God spoke light into darkness and revealed Himself. Abram's encounter with the Lord was so real that he left everything he had known, just like that. People he knew back in the day surely thought Abram was out of his mind. But I can just hear him say, "I may be crazy, but I have faith in God." We know the end of the story. Galatians 3:6-9 says:

> Abraham "believed God, and it was accounted to him for righteousness." Therefore know that only those who are of faith are sons of Abraham. And the Scripture, foreseeing that God would justify the Gentiles by faith, preached the gospel to Abraham beforehand, saying, "In you all the nations shall be blessed." So then those who are of faith are blessed with believing Abraham."

Abram started out strong with God and his legacy continues today. In like manner, you may not see everything God is doing at this moment, but if you'll trust Him, even when it seems crazy, He'll bring you all the way through. More than this, He'll build on your faith in future generations.

A week or two after I returned home from laying my son to rest, I had to minister at a funeral where a grief-stricken mother had lost her son. I said, "Wow, Lord . . . " But I had the words to say. I can't tell you how many children's funerals I've ministered over since that time. To my amazement, as the Lord would have it, I even ministered at the funeral for the six children who tragically drowned in Shreveport in August 2010. Each time God used me, I found that I was uniquely prepared to help those who were grieving and speak life into their situations. I can't explain it, but it's real.

I'm glad to say that I'm now in the stage where my memories of Larry are bringing me more joy than grief. However, there are times when I get emotional just thinking about him: like when I see my youngest son, Elijah, who looks just like him. Elijah has many of Larry's ways and mannerisms. He constantly reminds me of him. As a result, not a day goes by when I don't think about Larry III.

Sometimes I see different young men in church or at an event who favor my son, and it either brings great joy or a little sorrow, depending on where I am psychologically. That's why I took the time to go into great depth about managing your soul. Where you are, spiritually and emotionally, determines how you handle everyday life.

As you walk through the grief process, there will be times you'll be reminded of your loss. There may even be times God calls you to help someone else in a similar situation. So I encourage you, though it may cut close to your heart, be willing to move beyond your pain and obey Him. Stepping forward in spite of your grief often seems crazy, but in reality, it's a powerful expression of your faith. You may never know how your actions will impact the future, but believe me: God has it well in hand. So, my friend, trust Him and move forward.

We either let the pain consume us, or we consume the pain. It's our choice. Think of it this way. You can choose to be a thermometer or a thermostat. A thermometer rises and falls according to the outside environment. A thermostat creates an atmosphere—if it's set at seventy-three degrees, the entire house will stay at that temperature. It's important, as believers in Christ, for us to stand as thermostats, not as thermometers.

The Holy Spirit sets the atmosphere for us, and we, believing, follow and set the atmosphere around us. Although there will likely be many times that doing this seems crazy, by the grace of God, we can stand in faith and overturn all evidence to the contrary. We can be cool, calm, and collected in every situation.

COMING TO TERMS WITH THE WILL OF GOD

We may be troubled on every side, but how we handle our challenges depends on us, as we depend on God. Everyone has problems. It's how we see them, and then deal with them, that matters. Our responses and reactions to trouble really define who we are. Do we believe God, or do we believe in what we can do? Do we believe the Lord is working out our situation according to His will for our greater good, or do we try to determine our own destiny? Romans 8:28-29 and 31-32 in the *Amplified Bible* says:

> We are assured and know that [God being a partner in their labor] all things work together and are [fitting into a plan] for good to and for those who love God and are

called according to [His] design and purpose. For those whom He foreknew [of whom He was aware and loved beforehand], He also destined from the beginning [foreordaining them] to be molded into the image of His Son [and share inwardly His likeness], that He might become the firstborn among many brethren. . . . What then shall we say to [all] this? If God is for us, who [can be] against us? [Who can be our foe, if God is on our side?] He who did not withhold or spare [even] His own Son but gave Him up for us all, will He not also with Him freely and graciously give us all [other] things?

In light of this passage, let's discuss the will of God, shall we? Many times in life, especially when we experience loss, we question why God allows certain things to happen. So let's walk through some scriptures to get a general idea of what God's will is for us.

First of all, it is God's will for us to believe in Jesus Christ and have eternal life. John 3:16 says: "For God so loved the world that He gave His only begotten Son, that whoever believes in Him should not perish but have eternal life."

Second, it is the will of God for us to love Him, obey Him, and receive His Holy Spirit, who helps us and guides us through this life. Jesus said in John 14:15-17: "If you love Me, keep My commandments. And I will pray the Father, and He will give you another Helper, that He may abide with you forever—the Spirit of truth, whom the world cannot receive, because it neither sees Him nor knows Him; but you know Him, for He dwells with you and will be in you." (See also John 14:25-26 and16:7-15.)

Third, it is the Lord's will for us to abide in Him (manage our souls wisely) and be productive for His kingdom. In John 15:5, Jesus added: "I am the vine, you are the branches. He who abides in Me, and I in him, bears much fruit; for without Me you can do nothing." As we abide in the Lord through prayer, praise, and holy meditation, we express true worship unto the Lord. (See also John 4:23.)

Fourth, as we abide in Him, it is God's will to transform us into His image. Second Corinthians 3:17-18 says: "Now the Lord is the Spirit; and where the Spirit of the Lord is, there is liberty. But we all, with unveiled face, beholding as in a mirror the glory of the Lord, are being transformed into the same image from glory to glory, just as by the Spirit of the Lord."

Fifth, it is the will of God, as we abide in Him, to see eternally in the midst of our troubles. Second Corinthians 4:17-18 says: "For our light affliction, which is but for a moment, is working for us a far more exceeding and eternal weight of glory, while we do not look at the things which are seen, but at the things which are not seen. For the things which are seen are temporary, but the things which are not seen are eternal."

Next, it is God's will for all of His people to be one, so the world may believe He sent Jesus. In John 17:20-21 Jesus said: "I do not pray for these alone, but also for those who will believe in Me through their word; that they all may be one, as You, Father, are in Me, and I in You; that they also may be one in Us, that the world may believe that You sent Me." God wants us to love Him, and to love our neighbor as ourselves, so we'll be salt and light in a dying world. (See Mark 12:28-31 and Matthew 5:13-16.)

Finally, it is God's will to reward us. Jesus said in Revelation 22:12, "Behold, I am coming quickly, and My reward is with me, to give to every one according to his work." The Lord is faithful. He rewards us for every act of faith, not just at the end of this age but also during the course of our daily lives. But be careful! There are also rewards for the unbelieving and disobedient. When you have a chance, look up the word *reward* in your concordance. I assure you it will be an eye-opening experience.

There are many other scriptures that reveal the will of God to us. So it behooves us to have an intimate knowledge of the Word of God. That way, by the power of the Holy Spirit within us, we can apply His Word, which is His will, to our daily lives. If you'd like, you could start by reading Jesus' "Sermon on the Mount" (as it is widely known) to discover more about God's will and purpose for your life (Matthew 5–7).

But the bottom line is—*God loves us.* He made the supreme sacrifice and gave up His only begotten Son, so we could live the abundant life of faith. God cares about everything that concerns us and wants us to enjoy the benefits of eternal life, which starts when we receive Jesus. I mentioned one of these benefits in chapter 2 when I was sharing with you about my son's passing. The Holy Spirit gently reminded me of Psalm 61:1-4 and comforted my soul. Nothing can compare to receiving the Lord's comfort. When all evidence is to the contrary, He is a refuge of hope, strength, and peace.

IS THIS VICTORY, LORD?

An excellent example of being hard-pressed on every side and weathering paradoxes in our life of faith is David, the second king of Israel. David was no stranger to private pain. First of all, it appears there may have been some dysfunction in his family. When the prophet Samuel came to anoint the next king of Israel, David's father didn't even think about him but presented his seven brothers. Then when Samuel said none of them were God's choice, it was like his father said, "Oh, yeah . . . I have David." (See 1 Samuel 16:4-11.)

I wonder what David was thinking as he was minding the sheep, watching this play out. Then the scriptures say:

> So he sent and brought him in. Now he was ruddy, with bright eyes, and good-looking. And the LORD said, 'Arise, anoint him; for this is the one!' Then Samuel took the horn of oil and anointed him in the midst of his brothers; and the Spirit of the LORD came upon David from that day forward. (vv. 12-13)

Instantly, the least one in the family had become first. Think of how it might have been for young David to carry the knowledge of his calling and the weight of God's anointing. But we soon find out that David was a worshiper. Not long after he was anointed to be the next king of Israel, David was called to play soothing music for King Saul when the king was distressed. Then he became his "armorbearer" (1 Samuel 16:14-21). And he was anointed; whenever David played for Saul, the "distressing spirit would depart from [Saul]" (v. 23).

But Saul began to resent David after David killed Goliath and the women sang, "Saul has slain his thousands, and David his ten thousands." One day while David was ministering to Saul on the harp, the king threw a spear at him, saying "I will pin David to the wall!" (See 1 Samuel 18:7-11). The Bible says David escaped from him twice, but imagine the shock and grief he must have experienced. The person he had loved, honored, and taken care of for so long—the most powerful man in Israel—couldn't stand him. David couldn't even go home for help.

Think about the pain David suffered when his buddy, Jonathan, the son of Saul, was ripped out of his life (read 1 Samuel 20). Then later, when Jonathan died in battle with his father and two brothers (1 Samuel 31), the news was brought to David. The Bible says he and his men tore their clothes, mourned, wept, and fasted until evening (2 Samuel 1:11-12). What was David feeling? What was he going through?

David's life was a paradox. He was always on the run, yet doing the right thing in the eyes of the Lord. First Samuel 22 talks about how almost four hundred men approached David. They were in debt, discontented, and distressed (v. 2). These four hundred men obviously admitted they were suffering from private pain, low self-esteem, and so on. Why did they come to him? They knew his story. They knew his destiny, they saw his pain, and they joined him in purpose.

Notice David didn't pull back because he was in pain and refuse to lead them. He trusted God, although he was in pain, and reached out to help others. Psalm 78:72 says, "So [David] was their shepherd with an upright heart; he guided them by the discernment and skillfulness [which controlled] his hands" (AMP). David didn't let the pain consume him; he consumed the pain. As the Holy Spirit set the temperature in his heart, David chose to obey and stand as a thermostat, setting the atmosphere for those God had given to serve under his command.

I could go on and on about the grief David endured because of the anointing upon his life. Think about it. He didn't ask to be anointed. The Lord sent His prophet to him while he was doing his daily chores. I wouldn't doubt there were times David cried out to God, "Why do I have to suffer like this because of the anointing?" But yet, he loved the Lord and worshiped Him. David continually prayed, praised, and worshiped the Lord; He understood God knew better than he did and that his destiny was wrapped up in Him.

Now David wasn't perfect. I recall that, years later, he fell into sin by sleeping with Bathsheba, another man's wife, after David had become king of Israel. Just think of the pain he must have felt, knowing he had let the Lord down. To make matters worse, she got pregnant, and David sent orders for her husband to be killed in battle. After she had their son, the baby became ill. David fasted and prayed for seven days, but their baby son died. (See 2 Samuel 11–12:19.)

When David heard of this, he got up, washed himself, changed his clothes, and went to the house of the Lord to worship (v. 20). But the pain of losing his son was still fresh inside him. It speaks volumes that David chose to lean on and trust in God, in spite of his failures and his grief. But you see, God was working all things together for good. He had a purpose in mind that was much bigger than their pain.

After that situation passed, God had mercy on them both. He blessed David and Bathsheba with a second son, Solomon (v. 24). He grew up, assumed the throne of Israel, and became a very wise man. I'm a firm believer that God will bless you in your mess, as you turn it over to Him. Now, let me say that because of David's sin he had many troubles in his family (see 2 Samuel 12:1-15, especially vv. 9-14). I could name them all, but that would be a book in itself.

David had to deal with pain after pain, some that was undeserved and some that was the result of sin—but whatever David went through, he was a true worshiper. David had his moments, as we all do, but he never stopped praying, praising, and worshiping God. When I consider my own experience in light of everything David went through during his lifetime, I can only thank God for how gracious He's been to me.

I can say with confidence in the Lord that the more paradoxes we face, the stronger our faith can become. And I know this is easier said than done. But when you trust God, move beyond your pain, and obey Him, it becomes easier *when said and done.*

I understand why David prayed, "Let me hear of your unfailing love each morning, for I am trusting you. Show me where to walk, for I give myself to you. Rescue me from my enemies, LORD; I run to you to hide me. Teach me to do your will, for you are my God" (Psalm 143:8-10, NLT).

Some may not think that being able to make it through each day, simply because we can hear God's voice, is a posture of victory. But I beg to differ. Not only does God's unfailing love help us make it through the day, we can sleep better at night, even grieve more honestly and completely, because He's with us.

Yes, having faith in God often can often appear to be crazy, but it's the way He set things up to work according to His will. The Lord knows the end from the beginning, so let us trust Him. Although at times we may falter, God never fails. He's working all things together for good and sees our victory on the other side. He knows exactly when, according to His plan, He'll turn the tables on the enemy.

FAITH CHECK

Social philosopher and psychoanalyst Erich Fromm said, "To spare oneself from grief at all cost can be achieved only at the price of total detachment, which excludes the ability to experience happiness."[1] Well said. We can't avoid experiencing pain and loss; neither should we try to. We need to live, loving and trusting God and treasuring what He has given us. When challenges come we need to trust Him . . . again and again and again.

A life of faith is a life filled with paradoxes. So I pray that instead of letting grief consume you, you're choosing to believe God and consume your private pain. Now take some time alone, with your journal and pencil in hand, and work through the following questions.

1. Are you a spiritual thermometer or are you a thermostat? Has your private pain consumed you to the point that you can't function? If so, do this exercise. Write a list of the evidence that keeps confronting your mind. Leave a little space between items. When you're done, read over the list again, and then give each one to the Lord in prayer. When you finish, write in large letters over each item on your list: GOD IS GREATER.

2. Have you come to terms with the will of God concerning your situation? Why or why not? If you need to, go back and reread the section about coming to terms

with God's will. Do the supplementary reading, if time allows. Journal your thoughts.

Now let's close in prayer.

Faithful God and awesome King of the universe, we worship You as we enter Your presence. We thank You that from the beginning You established the principle that light overcomes darkness because it gives us hope we're coming all the way through our grief. We thank You that You have a master plan, that Your purposes never fail, and that You never leave or forsake us. We trust You, Lord. Thank You for putting hearts of faith within us. Lord, we declare by faith though we may be hard-pressed, we're not crushed. Although we may be perplexed, we're not in despair. And though we may be persecuted and struck down, we're not forsaken or destroyed because we belong to You. We accept Your will, Lord, trusting You're working all things together for our good. In the great name of Jesus we pray. Amen.

CHAPTER 8

SEEING THE LIGHT

Your Heavenly Treasure Chest

*It is the God who commanded light to shine out of darkness,
who has shone in our hearts to give the light of the knowledge of
the glory of God in the face of Jesus Christ. But we have this
treasure in earthen vessels, that the excellence of the power may
be of God and not of us.*

2 CORINTHIANS 4:6-7

I thank God that Jesus Christ is the life and light of my soul,
don't you? Now that we've taken some time to focus on
the process, let's refocus on the promise . . . Jesus Christ.
Because of what Christ has done, we can wake up each day
with renewed hope and strength, thanking God for His grace

and that His mercies are new every morning. In fact, I'm so grateful to have the Lord in my life I'd like to begin this chapter with a song . . . Psalm 121.

> I will lift up my eyes to the hills—
> from whence comes my help?
> My help comes from the LORD,
> who made heaven and earth.
> He will not allow your foot to be moved;
> He who keeps you will not slumber.
> Behold, He who keeps Israel
> shall neither slumber nor sleep.
> The LORD is your keeper;
> the LORD is your shade at your right hand.
> The sun shall not strike you by day,
> nor the moon by night.
> The LORD shall preserve you from all evil;
> He shall preserve your soul.
> The LORD shall preserve your going out and your coming in
> from this time forth, and even forevermore.

There are only eight verses in this biblical melody, but it's power-packed with promises . . . and it starts with a declaration we need to remember: *I will lift up my eyes*. Lifting up our eyes and seeing the light of Jesus is what gives us the strength, focus, and resolve to come all the way through the grief process. Having done this, there invariably comes a time when He lets us know we must lift up our eyes to Him and begin again.

Depending on where you are in your journey, that may sound like a tall order. But remember, there's a light inside of you: a treasure that can never be taken away. My friend, when you belong to God, your help comes from the Lord, the creator of the universe. His Word is filled with promises you can store in your heavenly treasure chest—your heart.

With this in mind, let's meditate on (think about) the Lord. Let's put a few more promises in our treasure chests, so we can open them just when we need it and remember nothing is impossible with God.

Jesus is the Word made flesh that was in the beginning with God. All things were made through Him (John 1:1-3). He is the "Seed" of the woman that bruises the head of the serpent (Genesis 3:15). Oh, yes! God always keeps His promises. He cursed the enemy of our souls, and promised he would eat dust and crawl on his belly all the days of his life (v. 14). I declare to you now in the name of Jesus Christ, Satan is under your feet.

In His wisdom, God fulfilled His Word to the letter. Jesus came to earth as a divine Seed placed in the womb of a young virgin, Mary. The angel Gabriel told her, "The Holy Spirit will come upon you, and the power of the Highest will overshadow you; therefore, also, that Holy One who is to be born will be called the Son of God" (Luke 1:35).

God Himself fertilized the woman's Seed supernaturally by the power of the Holy Spirit. In doing so, He reversed the curse of Adam and guaranteed that Jesus would one day strip the enemy of his power and restore humanity to Him. Oh, yes! Jesus has crushed the head of the enemy.

So lift up your eyes and see the Light! Isaiah 9:6-7 says:

> For unto us a Child is born,
> unto us a Son is given;
> and the government will be upon His shoulder.
> And His name will be called
> Wonderful, Counselor, Mighty God,
> Everlasting Father, Prince of Peace.
> Of the increase of His government and peace
> there will be no end,
> upon the throne of David and over His kingdom,
> to order it and establish it with judgment and justice
> from that time forward, even forever.
> The zeal of the LORD of hosts will perform this.

No matter what you've gone through and what your situation may be, in Jesus Christ you have victory over the enemy. You have a mighty ruler on your side who stands ready to come to your aid. Jesus is passionate about your deliverance. He died to give you life, peace, and victory.

As you hold on to faith in Jesus, you can let go of your pain, rise from the ashes of your loss, and move forward. Because God loves you and keeps His word, you are still more than able to lead a positive, productive life. Are you with me?

DO YOU COMPREHEND THE LIGHT?

Now, literally speaking, being able to see the light and comprehending it are two different things. It's much like being either a hearer or a doer of the Word (see James 1:22-25). John 1:5 says, "And the light [Jesus] shines in darkness, and the darkness did not comprehend it." In the Greek, the word *comprehend* means, "to take eagerly, i.e., seize, possess, etc."[1] Digging a little more deeply, it has a fuller meaning: "to lay hold of so as to possess as one's own, to appropriate."[2]

So Jesus is the life and the light of men, but unless we take hold of Him as our own and appropriate His promises, we stay in darkness. It is possible to walk in the light in one area, while still being in the dark in another. So I ask you: Do you comprehend the Light? Are you taking hold of Jesus and all He has for you so He can transform your private pain into public victory? If you're still in the process of taking hold of the hope and healing Jesus has for you, I pray that God would grant you grace to fully receive Him and be restored.

One day the Lord spoke to my heart, and I had to make a decision. I often say jokingly that the Lord "slapped me out of it." How? He took me right back to Calvary. He reminded me that He had also lost His Son. Think about it. God could have slain the world when He looked down upon the cross, but the "Treasure in the Darkness" when the earth turned black was Jesus.

Jesus' death brought salvation to the world. For this reason, during our times of darkness we can discover treasures in the dark, because Jesus has already been there. God is patient. In spite of all evidence to the contrary, He allowed everything to play out—because Jesus' pain had a purpose. He's the reason we can have hope in our challenges and be thankful that all things will work together for our good. Isaiah 53:2-5 says:

> For He shall grow up before Him as a tender plant,
> and as a root out of dry ground.
> *He has no form or comeliness;*
> and when we see Him,
> there is no beauty that we should desire Him.
> He is despised and rejected by men,
> *a Man of sorrows and acquainted with grief.*
> And we hid, as it were, our faces from Him;
> He was despised, and we did not esteem Him.
> *Surely He has borne our griefs*
> *and carried our sorrows;*
> Yet we esteemed Him stricken,
> smitten by God, and afflicted.
> But He was wounded for our transgressions,
> He was bruised for our iniquities;
> the chastisement of our peace was upon Him,
> *and by His stripes we are healed* [emphasis mine].

Let's consider this together. Jesus started out with no form or comeliness—much like the earth was "without form, and void" at the beginning of creation (Genesis 1:2). He had no beauty that we should desire Him. This not only is an uncanny parallel to the earth at the beginning of creation, it also clearly describes how we feel in the aftermath of a tragic loss. But Jesus, the light of the world, is well acquainted with grief. He carried our sorrows so we wouldn't have to struggle in the dark.

In the garden of Gethsemane, before He was crucified, Jesus (the Son of Man) prayed in anguish, "My Father! If it is possible, let this cup of suffering be taken away from me." Then He shifted and laid hold of His identity as the Son of God and said, "Yet I want your will to be done, not mine" (Matthew 26:39 NLT).

When Jesus was on the cross suffering intense pain and grief, darkness filled the land. The final battle between His spirit and His flesh was almost over. The Son of Man (His flesh) called out with a loud voice, " 'Eli, Eli, lema sabachthani?' which means 'My God, my God, why have you abandoned me?' " (See Matthew 27:46, NLT.) Then He shifted again and uttered His last words as the Son of God: "Father, into your hands I commit my spirit" (Luke 23:46 NIV) . . . and He breathed his last breath.

Jesus understands all too well what it means to suffer private pain. According to Isaiah 53:7, "He was oppressed and He was afflicted, yet He opened not His mouth; He was led as a lamb to the slaughter, and as a sheep before its shearers is silent, so He opened not His mouth." Jesus endured unbearable pain without saying a word . . . so that you could come all the way through the grief process. Jesus cares so much about how you feel that He gave His life for it.

Isaiah 53:10 continues: "Yet it pleased the LORD to bruise Him; He has put Him to grief. When You make His soul an offering for sin, He shall see His seed, He shall prolong His days, and the pleasure of the LORD shall prosper in His hand."

Let me put it this way. There's healing power in grief because Christ suffered on our behalf. Jesus willingly made Himself of no reputation, humbled Himself, and became obedient to the point of death so the Father's will could be accomplished—restoring us to Himself. But it gets better. Philippians 2:9-11 says:

> Therefore God also has highly exalted Him and given Him the name which is above every name, that at the name of Jesus every knee should bow, of those in heaven, of those on earth, and of those under the earth, and that every tongue should confess that Jesus Christ is Lord, to the glory of God the Father.

I say to you right now, your private pain and grief must bow to the name of Jesus! Do you receive it? Will you comprehend it and make it your own? Let me encourage you once again—*You Can Do All Things Through Christ!*

When God brought this back to me while I was grieving for my son, I had to pause and really take a look in my treasure chest (my heart). I said to myself, *Wait a minute; I know I'm suffering. I know I'm in pain, but the Lord knows how I feel. I can, I will come through this.* And though it didn't make sense to my natural mind, I leaned on the Word and came through in Jesus' name. I reached into my treasure chest and apprehended the Light.

I had been telling people for years, and still do, there's a reason for everything. As I dealt with my private pain, I was faced with either believing my own words or eating them— so I chose to believe them. There's a reason for everything. I may not ever understand why my son died, but I know there was a reason God allowed it to happen.

Perhaps one of the reasons may have been for me to write this book so that someone else—yes, even you—could be liberated. As I said before, I'm more focused than I've ever been on winning souls to the Lord by any means necessary. Through my son's death, many others are receiving new life. I'm glad that I listened to and believed my own teachings.

When your heart is overwhelmed ask God to lead you to the Rock (Psalm 61:2). I've had moments since my son's death when darkness tried to overwhelm me. But by the grace of God, I kept lifting my eyes to the Lord. He'll do the same for you. God understands your pain. He knows, just as sure as the sun shines, you'll have cloudy days. But when darkness comes, you can be assured the sun will shine again.

YOU CAN RISE UP FROM YOUR GRIEF

Jesus Christ, the light of the world, got up three days later on that great Resurrection morning with all authority in His hands. And so, again, though we must go through some painful situations, we can rise from every situation. We can be resurrected: spiritually, physically, financially, and emotionally as we trust God in those situations. I'm grateful to God that I can see and comprehend the true light, Jesus Christ. When He shines in our hearts (our treasure chests), He demonstrates who He is to us.

Second Corinthians 1:20-22 (NLT) says:

> For all of God's promises have been fulfilled in Christ with a resounding "Yes!" And through Christ, our "Amen" (which means "Yes") ascends to God for his glory. It is God who enables us, along with you, to stand firm for Christ. He has commissioned us, and he has identified us as his own by placing the Holy Spirit in our hearts as the first installment that guarantees everything he has promised us.

Truly, all we need is Jesus. He enables us to stand firm in the midst of trouble. He calls us by name, fills us with His Spirit, and equips us to do His work. So when we're weak or fall short of the glory of God, we can run to His throne of grace and receive mercy and grace to help in our time of need (see Hebrews 4:16).

Allow me to say to you what God imparted to my spirit: *you can snap out of it.* You can be restored, come to yourself again, and say, "I have to do something about my situation, because I don't want to remain as I am." Go deep in your chest of eternal treasures and take hold of what Christ has done for you. You can believe God and make a decision. You can make a choice to come all the way through the grief process.

I decided to find the treasure that was in the dark. And if I can do it, so can you! We can either take our time and enjoy the pity party or choose to snap out of it. I choose to be happy. How about you? I choose to go deep in my heart, find priceless treasure there, and make it my own. I choose to get better, to release my private pain, and keep moving forward.

There's a life lesson in every challenge. The lessons we learn prepare us for our next step. I believe that we graduate in life. We have levels. After every challenge, we go to a new level, where there are new types of challenges we have to face. With that being said, let us take on the mind-set that we're going to learn what God is teaching us for our next level.

Life is a journey. As we work through private pain, let's keep looking for the rich, hidden treasure of the Lord in our hearts. It helps us enjoy our lives and find meaning in our troubles.

I don't believe the Lord arbitrarily allows us to go through times of suffering. He's not a cold, distant figure sitting on a throne laughing at us; not at all. But there is a point to everything; both joy and sorrow are part of God's purpose for our lives because all things work together for our good. Not some things—all things. Knowing this, let's find the treasure in the dark and learn valuable lessons from our experiences.

Metaphorically speaking, I believe that every challenge we come through, trusting God, produces a treasure we can place in our crown.

Considering everything Jesus has done to help us overcome the challenges of life, I'll ask the question: *What are we not willing to give up for Jesus?* One of the most difficult parts of suffering loss is we're not ready to let go. But there's eternal treasure in our chest of promises to help us do what Christ gave up His life to accomplish. We are able to see His light and make it our own. We can let go of private pain and rise to a new level of faith.

Now remember this promise: "He who has begun a good work in you will complete it until the day of Jesus Christ" (Philippians 1:6). Jesus completed His work on Calvary so we could walk in newness of life. Believe it! Often, God delivers us *through*, not *out of*, our pain. By faith, we need to understand that God sometimes allows us to experience darkness to reveal the treasures in our heart. Each experience allows us to see God in a different light. As we keep our focus on the Lord in dark places, our pain can become our deliverance because He knows our name.

FAITH CHECK

A Chinese proverb says, "One joy shatters a hundred griefs."[3] When I think of Jesus, I say one joy shatters millions, even billions of griefs. He died "once for all" (Hebrews 10:10). As I close this chapter, I encourage you to take some time and really search your treasure chest. Think about how much the Lord Jesus Christ loves you. He is the treasure, the light, in your heart . . . and YOU are His treasure. Now, it's time to check your faith.

1. How well do you comprehend the light of Jesus? Sit down with your journal and pen; identify the areas in your heart where you may still be in darkness. Be totally honest with yourself. When you've finished writing your thoughts, take them to the Lord in prayer.
2. Are you ready to snap out of it and rise up from your pain? Why or why not? Consider your journey and write a few thoughts in your journal. Submit them to the Lord in prayer.
3. Bookmark this chapter, just like you did chapter 1. Keep both chapters at the top of your treasure chest.

They'll come in handy whenever you need to see the light and remind yourself of the treasure within you.

Now let's pray as we get ready to take the next step of faith.

Dear Lord Jesus, we thank You that we can lift up our eyes and see You, the light of our souls and the treasure of our hearts. We thank You that You're acquainted with grief and understand our sorrows. Help us rise up from private pain by the power of the Holy Spirit, like You rose from the grave. When You challenge us to let go of grief and begin again, help us snap out of it, Lord. Help us understand You have a reason for everything so we'll learn the lessons You have for us. We thank You, Lord, that all of God's promises are fulfilled in You. We lift our eyes to You, Jesus. Lead us to our next level of faith. Help us always be mindful of what You've done for us so we can eagerly possess Your promises. In Your name we pray. Amen.

CHAPTER 9

MOVING FORWARD

You Are a Light to the World

*Therefore we also, since we are surrounded by so great
a cloud of witnesses, let us lay aside every weight,
and the sin which so easily ensnares us, and let us run with
endurance the race that is set before us, looking unto Jesus, the
author and finisher of our faith, who for the joy that was set
before Him endured the cross, despising the shame, and has sat
down at the right hand of the throne of God.*

HEBREWS 12:1-2

Faith is the "substance," the confident assurance of things we hope for.[1] It is the "evidence" or proof of things we can't see with the natural eye.[2] (See Hebrews 11:1.) Our faith in God causes us to consistently rely upon

Jesus, the author and finisher of our faith. It gives us a firm conviction that's based upon hearing Him because we can't physically see Him in the earthly realm.[3] Faith is the "proving test" of what God has already done.[4] So, my friend, having done all, I urge you to stand. Hold on to your faith in God. Keep moving forward.

I applaud you for trusting the Lord and working through the grief process with me in this book. In doing so, you've been proving what He has already done in your life. Remember, the end depends upon the beginning. Don't just read this phrase, comprehend it. Take hold of it and make it your own. Keep it safe in your heavenly treasure chest so you can call upon it, and every other promise of God, when you need it.

You've come a long way since we started this journey of faith, and you may still have a way to go. But you can rest assured in God's promises. His works were finished from the foundation of the world (Hebrews 4:3); He prepared His kingdom from the foundation of the world (Matthew 25:34); and He chose you from before the foundation of the world (Ephesians 1:4). So take comfort. The very hairs on your head are numbered (Matthew 10:30).

You might wonder, if this is true, why there are so many paradoxes in life. Consider this with me. A paradox is a seemingly contradictory event or statement that expresses a possible truth.[5] I'm sure you've experienced many paradoxes, especially while coming through the grief process. But remember, a paradox only seems contradictory because it's based on facts you look at in the natural realm. However, when you see your private pain and your situation with the eyes of faith, the truth of your circumstances is revealed.

I want to emphasize: the paradoxes you experience are real. But how you perceive them makes all the difference— because that determines your response and your final outcome. Make it your priority as you move forward to believe God and see with the eyes of faith, all evidence to the contrary.

Now, believing God doesn't mean you deny your problems. Once you see, you have to keep it real, take off the public mask, and admit you have an issue. Let down your guard, pull down the images in your mind, and be transparent with the Lord and others. Be willing to get counsel and agreement in prayer. Healing will come.

When and if waiting gets tough, guard your treasure. Don't allow private pain to go unchecked or you'll fall into presumption. Believe God, manage your soul, and confess the truth. Humble yourself daily and be ready to go to war, both in the realm of the spirit and in your daily life. Do what you can do, and God will do what only He can do in your life. God doesn't need your help. He wants to be your silent partner and accomplish His will and purpose, both in and through you. Remember, real treasure endures.

As you come through the grief process, have no confidence in the flesh. In other words, don't let go of faith by allowing yourself to become self-confident about your progress. Keep coming to the Lord through prayer, praise, holy meditation, and true worship. Lift your eyes to Jesus. He gladly humbled Himself and gave up His life to be your Lord and deliverer.

Finally, don't entertain the enemy. Submit to God, resist the devil, and he'll run from you; it's a promise (James 4:7). Satan is a defeated foe. Jesus' finished work on the cross finished Satan for eternity. Our Lord has triumphed over the enemy. He has disarmed all principalities and powers and made a public spectacle of them (Colossians 2:15). Hebrews 2:14-15 adds: "Inasmuch as the children have partaken of flesh and blood, He Himself likewise shared in the same, that through death He might destroy him who had the power of death, that is, the devil, and release those who through fear of death were all their lifetime subject to bondage."

I don't know about you, but I'm having a praise party! Whenever I meditate on the Lord and His promises I want to sing songs of deliverance. Let's sing one together, shall we?

> I will sing to the LORD,
> for He has triumphed gloriously!
> The horse and its rider
> He has thrown into the sea!
> The LORD is my strength and song,
> and He has become my salvation;
> He is my God, and I will praise Him;
> my father's God, and I will exalt Him.

The LORD is a man of war;
the LORD is His name. (Exodus 15:1-3)

Of course, Moses and the children of Israel sang this song when God parted the Red Sea and delivered them out of the hands of Pharaoh and his army. But we can be thankful, come into His presence with singing, and bless His name. Our God is a mighty deliverer.

STAY THE COURSE

I bless the Lord that we can lay aside every weight, and the sin that so easily ensnares us, and stay the course for His glory. We can run with endurance the race that is set before us, looking unto Jesus, the author and finisher of our faith. We may not always conquer our pain, but we can stay in faith and overcome it through the Word of God.

Now, let's take stock of your journey while reading this book. How has this process matured you? You have likely endured a season of testing and warfare before you started reading. And there's a good chance certain sensitive areas may have been stirred up a little, especially when completing the Faith Check exercises. You can thank the Lord for having come this far, remaining in a state of dependency upon Him. Praise the Lord! This process has matured you.

I have encountered many people who were disappointed in themselves for the way they weathered their stormy season. Did you become disappointed in yourself, either before or while reading this book? Let me counsel you: *But God!* I imagine when Peter stepped out in faith onto that stormy water, but then began to sink, he felt disappointed that the storm seemed bigger than Jesus (Matthew 14:22-33). He was probably mortified when he denied Jesus three times on the night before He was crucified (Mark 14:66-72). I say to you: God understands our weaknesses.

Psalm 8:3-4 says: "When I consider your heavens, the work of Your fingers, the moon and the stars, which You have ordained, what is man that You are mindful of him, and the son of man that You visit him?" Our God who formed all of creation, who is able to keep the celestial bodies in their places, who sustains the entire universe by the Word of His power, is never put off by our weaknesses. The same Lord who stretched out His hand to keep Peter from sinking has His hand outstretched to You. You are never alone and without a deliverer.

If you have any regrets, take a moment now and deal with them. It's that simple with the Lord. You may have stumbled and faltered in the proving test of what God has already done for you, but you're never too far from His rescue and love. Just keep coming to Him. Come boldly before His throne of grace. He will be merciful and give you grace to help in your time of need. The Lord is quick to forgive and restore.

So lift your eyes! Your help comes from the Lord, the Maker of heaven and earth. He watches over you, knowing the end from the beginning, waiting with expectancy to speak life into darkness. You have a mighty deliverer!

LEND A HELPING HAND

We are His workmanship (Ephesians 2:10). We are all works in progress, and we are fearfully and wonderfully made (Psalm 139:14). So stay the course. The more you believe God and overcome, the more you can help others. When the Lord puts His light within you, He wants you to shine brightly so others can see it.

How can you shine when you're yet working through private pain? Second Corinthians 1:3-4 says that our "Father of mercies . . . comforts us in all our tribulation, that we may be able to comfort those who are in any trouble, with the comfort with which we ourselves are comforted by God." When the Lord comforts you, you become able to help someone else. And remember, a little dab will do you.

It might seem a little crazy to help someone else when you're still coming through your own grief process—but I found God gives us just what we need when we need it. You can really help people if you're moving forward in your process to become healthy. Think about it. There are some medical doctors who are sick themselves, but they still help others. You can do the same.

So, it's important for you to take care of yourself. Self-preservation is key—because you can't help someone else if you're deteriorating. So stay the course. Manage your soul, and you'll come out stronger than when you began. Think of your private pain as a teacher. The challenges you've weathered prepare you to help somebody else come through the grief process.

This reminds me of an illustration I often share about a ferocious lion and a tiny little mouse. Quickly stated, the lion was out of sorts because it had a thorn in its paw. The mouse saw the thorn, pulled it out, and they became good friends. There are a lot of angry people in the world, even in the church, because they're suffering from some sort of pain. The real problem is no one is pulling the thorn out of their paw. Instead, we often make things worse by judging, excluding, and isolating them. That isn't God's way of doing things, don't you agree?

Some people go around wearing a frown and don't speak to anyone. This doesn't mean they're mean or evil. It simply means they're probably dealing with something you don't know about, something they don't feel comfortable sharing with you. But instead of judging them, open your heart. Hear them out. Pray for them. Put yourself in a position where they can trust you. Then when they're confident enough to let go of their pain, they can cry on your shoulder and begin their healing process.

There's a way to reach out. If you recall, when the Lord prompted me to release my private pain during my radio program and in church that Sunday in 2011, it loosened the thorn in the paws of many. And that day, many hurting people began the healing process.

When you receive the healing touch of the Lord, you can tell the world it's real. And when you see someone else who is challenged, you can look that person in the eye and say, "Hey, I might not be feeling what you're feeling, but I understand. Truly, I understand." Lending a helping hand can be just that simple.

I'll say it again: Pain doesn't discriminate. It hits you like a bullet, whether you're titled or not. But I have a special burden for those who have titles. There have been times that I've asked the Lord, "Who does the one that everyone bleeds on bleed on?" In other words, who can they open up to and be real with about their feelings?

There are people on every level of church ministry who are suffering from private pain: pastors, evangelists, choir members, Sunday school teachers, ushers, and so on. In the greater community, there are fathers, mothers, elder children—anyone who feels responsible for others—who need a compassionate shoulder to cry on from time to time. Who can these people bleed on?

I oftentimes say to leaders that it's important to bleed up. That's why I said before that every pastor needs a pastor. Other leaders in the church need to go to a trusted peer, or the pastor, to pour out their hearts. We all need each other. Again, that's why it's so important to keep it real. We can't afford to let the enemy steal our treasure. I encourage you to be that shoulder, that trustworthy person that someone else can bleed on.

Have you noticed when a preacher falls from grace that the whole community is shocked? The general attitude seems to be that people who sit in the pews can go through difficulties but not so those in the pulpit. If a leader isn't the picture of health, his or her followers will often judge, lose respect for, and even replace him or her. I think that's a double standard.

Granted, a preacher is called and anointed of God and is held to a higher biblical standard, but he or she isn't Jesus. We're all on a journey. We're all works in progress on our way home to eternity. So we need to keep it real and be there for each other. If it's one hundred degrees outside, it's the same temperature for everyone—sinner, saint, preacher . . . everybody. I can catch a cold just like you can. Leaders aren't immune to private pain simply because we're called into ministry. We're human, just like everyone else.

Let us learn to listen more and be compassionate. Let us pray for each other and keep confessing the truth to one another.

This brings a story to mind. In Genesis 35:16-18, Jacob's wife Rachel was in hard labor while giving birth to their son Benjamin. As she was dying she named the baby "Ben-Oni," which means "son of my sorrow."[6] But his father changed his name to Benjamin, which means "son of (the) right hand."[7]

Because of her pain, Rachel, the wife of the next patriarch of Israel, confessed her pain instead of the promise. But Jacob, who had been renamed Israel, confessed that Benjamin was "the son peculiarly dear to me." According to Psalm 80:17, the man of the right hand is one who is much loved and regarded of God.[8] So you see, Rachel shows us that even those in the ranks of leadership can be in pain and stumble. And Jacob, whose faith had been tried and proven not long before, shows us the love and mercy of God.

This story also raises another issue we should remember as we work through private pain. Oftentimes, when we go through challenges, we say things that are unhealthy for others. How many parents today are causing grief in their children's lives because of their pain? How many pastors are speaking from the pulpit and hurting people because they're struggling with issues? Like I said before, hurting people hurt people and healthy people help people.

When we're consumed with pain, we can fly off the handle, be flippant with our words, and create pain for others. Some of us do this subconsciously, and others do it consciously. If we're not careful, unchecked private pain can have a domino effect. We need to submit ourselves to the Lord, resist the devil and consume the pain so others can be spared unnecessary grief.

Going back to Rachel and Jacob, the Lord made sure the negative label didn't go into effect in Benjamin's life. The hidden treasure in that situation shined from within

Jacob/Israel, who had once been a schemer and had stolen his brother Esau's birthright. But God had allowed Jacob to go through a process that had proven his faith, and he had been transformed. This prepared him to speak life instead of death. We always need people in our lives who speak life to us, especially when we're in pain, so we'll be able to rise up and change our situations.

If you're suffering today because of an issue with one or both of your parents, there is help for you. Perhaps you've become an overachiever because subconsciously you feel like you're not good enough. But if you'll open up and expose your pain, you'll find there are many who have been belittled. In fact, many overachievers would probably tell you that someone told them they weren't going to amount to anything.

But the blessing is, though Rachel spoke sorrow upon him, Benjamin's future was literally changed because Jacob/Israel spoke life. In kind, there are some Ben-Oni's in the world who need someone to give them an uplifting word so their name can be changed to Benjamin. That person could be you. If you're hurting, the person who speaks life to you could be a loved one, a good friend, your pastor, or even a professional counselor.

It's extremely important for us to find positive people who can speak life into our situation and tell us who we are and who we're not so we can stop believing the devil's lies. I don't know where I would have been if I hadn't had positive people surrounding me. Not everyone has that blessed privilege.

So, again, self-preservation by managing your soul is necessary in the day-to-day process of proving your faith. Think of it this way. On a plane, the flight attendant routinely gives instructions during the preflight briefing. If the cabin pressure suddenly drops and there's a loss of oxygen, an oxygen mask will automatically fall down out of the compartment above you.

The attendant explains the first thing you need to do is secure your mask before you help anyone else. That makes total sense. If you don't secure your mask first, and then try to help someone else, you could both lose consciousness and both of you would suffer. So, by all means, make sure to manage your soul as you come through the grief process; then you'll be able to help somebody else so they can survive their painful situation.

HAVE HOPE FOR THE FUTURE

I trust and pray that you're now experiencing more light and life in your situation. But bear in mind that doesn't mean you've come all the way through the process; however, it certainly means that you're headed in the right direction. I encourage you to look in the mirror and celebrate yourself. Appreciate yourself. Although you may still be facing some challenges, you're still alive. You're still breathing. You're still moving forward.

Imagine your life playing out on an EKG machine . . . as long as there's a heartbeat, it shows little bleeps that go up and down. When you have ups and downs, it simply means that you're still alive. There's still hope for tomorrow. In fact, there's an even greater hope we can all look forward to as children of God. So look in the mirror and celebrate yourself for being alive. Celebrate and praise God because you've made it this far. You've carried a heavy load, and now you're releasing it. You're laying aside that weight that once kept you in bondage so you can run the race God has set before you. You're heading into a new and improved life.

One day we'll all move forward into an incredible future. First Peter 1:3-8 says:

> Blessed be the God and Father of our Lord Jesus Christ, who according to His abundant mercy has begotten us again to a living hope through the resurrection of Jesus Christ from the dead, to an inheritance incorruptible and undefiled that does not fade away, reserved in heaven for you, who are kept by the power of God through faith for salvation ready to be revealed in the last time.

> In this you greatly rejoice, though now for a little while if need be, you have been grieved by various trials, and that the genuineness of your faith, being much more precious than gold that perishes, though it is tested by fire, may be found to praise, honor, and glory at the revelation of Jesus Christ, whom having not seen you love. Though now you do not see Him, yet believing, you rejoice with joy inex-

pressible and full of glory, receiving the end of your faith—
the salvation of your souls.

Wow. I don't know about you, but I'm getting ready to
have another praise party. Let me share with you a little
about what's ahead for us. There is yet another milestone
event coming when God will dramatically separate light from
darkness. This is our future hope, when we'll receive the
treasure to come.

Let me start by saying the devil, the enemy of our souls,
will be thrown into a pit for a thousand years. Then some-
time afterward, he'll be cast into the lake of fire and brim-
stone where the antichrist (the beast) and the false prophet
will be. Then the Word of God says they will all be tor-
mented forever and ever (read the entire passage in
Revelation 20:7-10).

It gets better. Revelation 21 opens up with John seeing a
magnificent vision of a new heaven and a new earth. Then he
saw the holy city, New Jerusalem, coming down out of
heaven from God (vv. 1-2). In the third verse, a loud voice
from heaven declared an awesome promise:

> "Behold, the tabernacle of God is with men, and He will
> dwell with them, and they shall be His people. God
> Himself will be with them and be their God. And God will
> wipe away every tear from their eyes; there shall be no
> more death, nor sorrow, nor crying. There shall be no
> more pain, for the former things have passed away." Then

He who sat on the throne said, "Behold, I make all things new." And He said to me, "Write, for these words are true and faithful."

Did you see that? All pain will be gone and all tears will be wiped away forever. Death will be a thing of the past. Sorrow will no longer exist. This sounds too good to be true! But I beg to differ. This is absolute truth. Do you believe it? More importantly, do you comprehend it? I declare to you today that when we take hold of Jesus, the author and finisher of our faith, we make this promise our own.

Now hold on, because it gets even better. The promise continues in Revelation 21:6-7: "And He said to me, 'It is done! *I am the Alpha and the Omega, the Beginning and the End. I will give of the fountain of the water of life freely to him who thirsts. He who overcomes shall inherit all things,* and I will be his God and he shall be My son'" [emphasis mine].

I say to you that not only can you overcome your private pain and come all the way through your grief process; in the name of Jesus, you can overcome every obstacle in this life— *because the end depends upon the beginning.* I want to see you there, my friend. I want to walk along the banks of the water of life with you, rejoicing when I hear your triumphant testimony. God made you a promise. When you overcome, you shall inherit all things.

Let me add another fantastic promise. Just before He went to be crucified, Jesus said to His disciples:

Let not your heart be troubled; you believe in God, believe also in Me. In My Father's house are many mansions; if it were not so, I would have told you. I go to prepare a place for you. And if I go and prepare a place for you, I will come again and receive you to Myself; that where I am, there you may be also. (John 14:1-3)

I want to point out two things. First, I trust you have received Jesus Christ as your personal Lord and Savior. That means *you* are His disciple. This promise also belongs to you. Second, notice Jesus didn't say, "I'm going to suffer and be crucified, and then afterward I'll return to the Father and prepare a place for you." Jesus was joyfully seeing beyond the pain He was about to endure. And not only this: He was speaking life and light so the disciples could see and take hold of their promising future.

I didn't mention this earlier, but I'd like to now. There's another reason our friend who sang at her mother's funeral experienced joy as she shared with her family in the limousine while en route to the church. Only months before, the Lord had graciously allowed her to lead her mother to Jesus Christ. He also lovingly confirmed to her after she cried out to Him a week or so later that her mother was eternally healthy and happy in an exceedingly better place.

You can be a witness, even in the midst of your pain. Would you allow Jesus to use you, even if it doesn't make sense to your natural mind? I exhort you again to open up, release your pain, and be used of God to make an eternal

difference in someone else's life. Because there are also promises for those who choose not to believe in and receive Christ.
You can read about them in Revelation 20 and 21. Read both
chapters in their entirety. No one, absolutely no one, needs
to suffer the grief and torment of being eternally separated
from God.

Now that you've read this book and have, I hope, applied
the principles of God's Word to your situation, you can come
in sync with God, His Word, and your assignment. The enemy
may have stolen from you and caused you grief, but you can
go on the offensive. You can join me and others in winning as
many souls to Christ as God will allow. And may I remind
you, the scriptures say He's not willing for ANY to perish, but
for ALL to have everlasting life (John 3:16).

So let your light shine, my friend. Let it shine, shine, shine.
You can snap out of it and enjoy your life to the fullest. I
exhort you to be happy! You can trust God and make things
work for you and your loved ones because He's working all
things together for your good! Trust God, keep moving forward, and be a producer. Make things happen, instead of
waiting for things to happen. God not only wants you to be
free from grief, He also has called you to rule and reign with
Him. There's no better time than the present to begin prepar-
ing for our magnificent future.

Let me leave you with yet another powerful promise from
the Father. Revelation 22:1-5 says:

And He showed me a pure river of water of life, clear as crystal, proceeding from the throne of God and of the Lamb. In the middle of its street, and on either side of the river, was the tree of life, which bore twelve fruits, each tree yielding its fruit every month. The leaves of the tree were for the healing of the nations.

And there shall be no more curse, but the throne of God and of the Lamb shall be in it, and His servants shall serve Him. They shall see His face, and His name shall be on their foreheads. There shall be no night there: They need no lamp nor light of the sun, for the Lord God gives them light. And they shall reign forever and ever.

There are enduring treasures in the dark on this side of heaven because God's eternal light will shine for eternity. His light is so brilliant it can shine to everyone around us, so they'll want to experience the same light and life they see in us. And tomorrow, my friend, we'll bask in the glory of God's presence for eternity.

I'll tell you what: If I don't see you on this side of heaven, my prayer for you is that you'll let your light shine for the glory of God. I have the same divine assurance in my heart for you that I have for my son Larry III . . . I know I'll see you in the morning.

So I encourage you, and I speak prophetically over your life that better days are ahead for you. What's coming for you, indeed, is much better than what has been. I'll leave you for now with the same words Moses spoke to the Israelites before God delivered them through the Red Sea.

Do not be afraid. Stand still, and see the salvation of the LORD, which he will accomplish for you today. For the Egyptians [the enemy and his minions] whom you see today, you shall see again no more forever. The LORD will fight for you, and you shall hold your peace. (Exodus 14:13-14)

And the Red Sea parted. Can you see the parting with the eyes of faith?

I say to you that your Red Sea has parted. You're moving forward, and you won't see the pain and grief that you've experienced anymore. You'll remember it differently, and the sting will be gone because you're releasing it. Now you can stand still and see the salvation of our God as He delivers you from private pain. You can take hold of your deliverance and cross over to the other side of grief.

This is your time to celebrate, as Miriam did with the tambourine, because you're going to see the schemes of the enemy destroyed in your life. So, my friend, I exhort you to lift your eyes and see your victory on the other side. Pursue God and move forward. All is well.

FAITH CHECK

Hilary Stanton Zunin said, "The risk of love is loss, and the price of loss is grief—but the pain of grief is only a shadow when compared with the pain of never risking love."[9] In the beginning when God created the heavens and the earth, and the Word was with God (and was God), He took the ultimate risk of love. He loved you so much that He created man in His own image. His love for you spanned the generations until He sent His only begotten Son, Jesus Christ, the second Adam, to reverse the curse forever.

Then Jesus, filled with passion for your soul, surrendered Himself to death on the cross . . . for He's not willing for any to perish but for all to have everlasting life. And let me remind you: He wants to be your silent partner. Would you come in sync with the Lord to see His will and purpose established, both in you and through you? I trust your answer will be a resounding yes.

As I prepare to close our journey together, I challenge you to rise up, be healed, and give yourself a lifelong challenge. How many souls can you win for Jesus Christ? How many people can you help who are still drowning in the sea of despair? I say to you: You are more than equal to the challenge. You are an overcomer. You don't have to be afraid of the dark. The light of eternal life is within you.

Now give me the joy of praying with you once again:

Dear Master, Lord, and Faithful Father, I come to You with my dear friend in the precious name of Jesus. We thank You for putting such rich treasure, Your eternal life and light, in our souls and for giving us the gift of faith to believe You and stay the course. We love You, Lord. We come into agreement with Your Word that we will lay aside every weight, and the sin that so easily ensnares us, and run with endurance the race You have set before us— lifting our eyes to You. Thank You for healing and delivering us from private pain and for bringing us all the way through the grief process. Lord, give us the wisdom and strength to comfort others with the same comfort we have received from You. As we shine our light to those around us, we thank You for doing what only You can do. Save, heal, and deliver, Lord. Use us for Your glory. We will give You all the praise and honor, for You are our strength and our song. Lord, You are a man of war who defeats the enemy every time. We declare to You that as we move forward, we will stand and see Your salvation. We thank You for it in Your glorious, excellent, and matchless name. Amen.

NOTES

CHAPTER 1

1. Ellie McGrath with reporting by Constance E. Richards, "Welcome, Freshmen!" September 10, 2001. www.time.com/time/magazine/article/9,9171,1000721,00.html. Accessed 2/21/2013.

2. L. Lawrence Brandon, *30 Minutes in Prayer: Entering God's Presence through Prayer, Praise, Holy Meditation & True Worship* (Shreveport: LLB Publishing, 2012), 10–11.

CHAPTER 2

1. Washington Irving, thinkexist.com/quotation/there_is_a_sacredness_in_tears_they_are_not_the.html. Accessed 2/21/2012.

CHAPTER 3

1. John Maxwell, thinkexist.com/quotation/people_do_not_care_how_much_you_know_ until_they/346868.html. Accessed 3/9/13.

2. Turkish Proverb, thinkexist.com/quotation/he_that_conceals_his_ grief_finds_no_remedy_for/163985. Accessed 3/9/13.

CHAPTER 4

1. "Sick" (2470, "lâ," Heb.) in the *Strong's Talking Greek and Hebrew Dictionary*. WORDsearch 7.0. Copyright © 2007 WORDsearch Corp. All rights reserved.

2. "Sick" (Vine's #1 / 2470, "lâ," Heb.) in *Vine's Expository Dictionary of Old and New Testament Words*. Ibid.

3. Benjamin Franklin, thinkexist.com/quotation/those_things_that_hurt_instruct/ 146116. Accessed 3/19/13.

CHAPTER 5

1. Steinmetz, Sol, et al. *Webster's American Family Dictionary*, "grief" (New York: Random House, 1998), 416. [dictionary.reference.com/browse/grief]. Accessed 3/10/13.

2. Grief, "Five Stages Theory," en.wikipedia.org/wiki/Grief. Accessed 3/10/13.

3. "Delivereth" (KJV, 5337, "n al," Heb.) in the *Strong's Talking Greek and Hebrew Dictionary*. WORDsearch 7.0. Copyright © 2007 WORDsearch Corp. All rights reserved.

4. "Deliver, rescue, save" (1404 / 5337, "n al," Heb.) in the *Theological Wordbook of the Old Testament*. Ibid.

5. "Serenity Prayer," Reinhold Neibuhr, en.wikipedia.org/wiki/Serenity_Prayer. Accessed 3/10/13.

6. Bishop Richard White and Evangelist Twinkie Clark, "Accept What God Allows." www.youtube.com/watch?v=KZTHaDJN-I. Accessed 3/10/13.

7. Elbert Hubbard, thinkexist.com/quotation/the_cure_for_grief_is_motion/ 144458.html. Accessed 3/10/13.

CHAPTER 6

1. Steinmetz, Sol, et al. *Webster's American Family Dictionary*, "circumstantial" (New York: Random House, 1998), 173.

2. Ibid.

3. L. Lawrence Brandon, *30 Minutes in Prayer: Entering God's Presence through Prayer, Praise, Holy Meditation & True Worship* (LLB Publishing, Shreveport, Louisiana, 2012), 17.

4. Jeff Wickwire, *Let the Journey Begin: First Steps for New Christians* (Shreveport: LLB Publishing), 39.

5. Brandon, *30 Minutes in Prayer*, 37.

6. John Adams, thinkexist.com/quotation/grief_drives_men_into_habits_of_ serious/184486.html. Accessed 3/11/13.

CHAPTER 7

1. Erich Fromm, thinkexist.com/quotation/to_spare_oneself_from_grief_at_all_cost_can_be/180893.html. Accessed 3/11/13.

CHAPTER 8

1. "Comprehended" (KJV, 2638, "katalamban ," Gk.) in the *Strong's Talking Greek and Hebrew Dictionary*. WORDsearch 7.0. Copyright © 2007 WORDsearch Corp. All rights reserved.

2. "Comprehended" (Vine's #1 / KJV, 2638, "katalamban," Gk.) in *Vine's Expository Dictionary of Old and New Testament Words*. Ibid.

3. Chinese Proverb, thinkexist.com/quotation/one_joy_shatters_a_hundred/185331.html. Accessed 3/11/13.

CHAPTER 9

1. "Substance" (5287, "hypostasis," Gk.) in the *Strong's Talking Greek and Hebrew Dictionary*; (Vine's #4 / 5287, "hypostasis," Gk.) in *Vine's Expository Dictionary of Old and New Testament Words*. WORDsearch 7.0. Copyright © 2007 WORDsearch Corp. All rights reserved.

2. "Evidence" (1650, "elenchos," Gk.) in the *Strong's Talking Greek and Hebrew Dictionary*. Ibid.

3. "Faith" (4102, "pistis," Gk.) in the *Strong's Talking Greek and Hebrew Dictionary*. (Vine's #1 / 4102, "pistis," Gk.) in *Vine's Expository Dictionary of Old and New Testament Words*. Ibid.

4. "Evidence" (Vine's #A-1 / 1650, "elegmos," Gk.) in *Vine's Expository Dictionary of Old and New Testament Words*. Ibid.

5. Steinmetz, Sol, et al. *Webster's American Family Dictionary*, "paradox" (New York: Random House, 1998), 687.

6. "Benoni" (KJV, 1126, "ben`ônî," Heb.) in the *Strong's Talking Greek and Hebrew Dictionary*. Ibid.

7. "Benjamin" (1144, "biny mîn," Heb.) in the *Strong's Talking Greek and Hebrew Dictionary*. Ibid.

8. Genesis 35:18. (from Psalm 80:17, "man of Your right hand") in *Adam Clarke's Commentary*. Ibid.

9. Hilary Stanton Zunin, thinkexist.com/quotation/the_risk_of_love_is_loss_and_the_price_of_loss_is/163074.html. Accessed 3/11/13.

REFLECTION / DISCUSSION QUESTIONS

for

Treasures in the Darkness

by Bishop L. Lawrence Brandon

Grief and loss are universal issues often masked behind frustration and anger. Whatever the source of your pain, Bishop Brandon's story is proof that God is ever-present in the hurt. The following reflection / discussion questions will help you take the next step on your own journey to find the gift of treasure in the darkness.

1. What is your private pain? Maybe your pain is raw and close to the surface. Maybe your pain is buried so deeply that it is hard to remember all the details, but the pain never stops. Name your pain and bring it forward so you can offer it to God.

2. Bishop Brandon says, "The end depends on the beginning." Think back on the beginning of your relationship with Christ. We know he is ever faithful, but sometimes we can forget in the face of our own darkness. Remember that time, and remind yourself of how much Jesus loves you then and now.

3. When Bishop Brandon finally was able to share his grief about his son's death, he was overwhelmed at the response of others who were blessed by his testimony. How has someone else's experience been a blessing to you? How can you share your private pain with another in a way that will be a blessing to you both?

4. Are you wearing a public mask? Perhaps the better question is, What is the mask you are wearing? How can you be more honest with yourself and others? What is the risk of dropping your mask? Could the reward be even greater?

5. Waiting on the Lord can be one of the hardest things we are called to do as Christians. Bishop Brandon was tempted to take matters into his own hands to avenge the death of his son, but he trusted God instead. Have you ever taken matters into your own hands? What were the

consequences? How can you wait upon the Lord in your present situation?

6. Bishop Brandon identifies eight stages of grieving for whatever you have lost that is causing you private pain:
   - Stage One: Shock and Denial
   - Stage Two: Pain, Guilt, and Frustration
   - Stage Three: Anger and Bargaining
   - Stage Four: Depression, Reflection, and Loneliness
   - Stage Five: The Upward Turn
   - Stage Six: Reconstruction and Working Through
   - Stage Seven: Acceptance and Hope
   - Stage Eight: A New Beginning

   How are you working through each stage of grief? Think about your own situation and look at the list to see where you are in the process. Remember that this is a journey you are not taking alone. Jesus is right beside you, even in the hardest times.

7. We know God is faithful to us. How can you receive His ongoing blessing and comfort as you heal from your private pain? Are you seeking His Word? Are you spending time in prayer? Perhaps you need to sit with a godly counselor to work through your hurt. How can you receive God's grace every day?

8. What is the will of God? It is easy to be angry with God when we suffer loss, but Bishop Brandon's reflections on what is the will of God remind us of God's sovereignty

and blessing in every situation. When you reflect on all the examples of God's will in chapter 7, how has God blessed you and been faithful?

9. Jesus faced death for our sins and was restored. He is our light in all things. Are you ready to receive His perfect healing and go forward? The answer may be no, at least for now. But know that He is there and His hand is reaching out to you. Jesus is the light that is within us, that overshadows any darkness. Receive Him and share His light.

BISHOP L. LAWRENCE BRANDON

Psalm 37:23 says, "The steps of a good man are ordered by the LORD." This clearly describes the life and ministry of Bishop L. Lawrence Brandon. A popular lecturer and the author of several books, including *Holiness Is Still Right, You Complete Me, A Faith That Feels Like Lying,* and *Thirty Minutes in Prayer,* Bishop Brandon is a well-loved pastor, minister, spiritual father, and community leader. As Senior Pastor and CEO of several churches, Bishop Brandon over-sees Praise Temple Full Gospel Baptist Cathedral, one of the fastest-growing congregations in the Shreveport/Bossier City, Louisiana, area. Covered in ministry by Bishop Paul S. Morton, Sr., the Presiding Bishop of the Full Gospel Baptist Church Fellowship, International (FGBCFI), Bishop Brandon is also the founder and CEO of Praise Temple Ministries and L. L. Brandon Ministries, Inc.

A socially active leader, businessman, and minister, Bishop Brandon serves as the Chair/CEO of the Northwest Louisiana Church Chamber of Commerce, Chairman of the Shreveport Airport Authority, and the Chair/CEO of the Board of the Northwest Louisiana Community Development Corporation. He is a seasoned member of various boards of directors, including the Goodwill Industries of Northwest Louisiana, the Council for the Advancement of Social Services and Education, the Shreveport Rescue Mission and "Fit for Life" Campaigns, the United Way Louisiana, Northwest Louisiana Region, and the Council for the Advancement of Social Services and Education. In January 2010, Mayor Cedric B. Glover recommended and appointed Bishop Brandon to the Shreveport Airport Authority Board, which was confirmed by the City Council. Bishop Brandon is the Managing Partner of Brandon Group International, LLC.

Having received numerous certifications, awards, and proclamations, Bishop Brandon is a member of the American Association of Christian Counselors and has also served as a Certified Pastoral Addiction Counselor (CPAC) for the National Board of Addiction Examiners. Certified by the

United States Air Force and the Louisiana State Board as a Substance Abuse Counselor, Bishop Brandon has served as a member of the Board of Directors for Louisiana's "One Church, One Addict" program.

A graduate of the Summer Leadership Institute '99 at Harvard University in Cambridge, Massachusetts, Bishop Brandon has earned a Bachelor of Arts Degree in Business Administration and received an Honorary Doctorate Degree in Divinity from Baptist Christian University of Shreveport, Louisiana. In addition, he has an earned a Master of Theology Degree from Guadalupe Baptist Theological Seminary of San Antonio, Texas, and is the recipient of an Honorary Doctorate in Humanities from Louisiana Baptist University. Bishop Brandon is pursuing a Master's Degree in Divinity at Oral Roberts University in Tulsa, Oklahoma.

Among his many accomplishments, Bishop Brandon received the honor to serve as a panel guest for the Social Security Reform Effort during President George W. Bush's visit to Shreveport in March 2005. On November 23, 2010, he earned the distinction of being unanimously recommended and approved by the Shreveport City Council to have Hutchinson Street in Shreveport dedicated in his name.

Bishop Brandon and his wife, affectionately known as Co-Pastor Wanda, joyfully serve together in ministry, and they have three children.

For other fine books, visit AbingdonPress.com